Evangelism in a Post-Christian Culture

Teach Yourself to Share the Gospel

Dr Alastair Ferrie

iUniverse, Inc.
New York Bloomington

Other Works by this author:

Step-by-Step: Aftercare for New Christians
(2004), published by iUniverse.

Acknowledgements:

I acknowledge the assistance and encouragement of Tony Coffey whose books, ministry and presence in our home over the years have served as a constant encouragement of the realness of the gospel message. Also a number of others have kindly read the manuscript and made helpful comments including: Max Dauner, Fred Jewell, John Renwick, Bob Webb, Frank Worgan, David Young, and Richard Youngblood.

I acknowledge the constant support and encouragement of my wife Linda and children Susan, Colin, Mark, Paula and Craig. When in the depths of the deepest valleys, it has been their constant support and belief in me that has inspired me to keep turning back to Him who is the head, from whom flow all blessings spiritual and physical. If ever someone has been blessed by a family who love and support, I have and I am of all men most blessed.

This book is dedicated to all those who will commit their lives to sharing the gospel of Christ. It is the book I wish someone had handed me thirty years ago as I began my ministry, and encapsulates some of the lessons I have taken years to learn with many struggles along the way.

Contents

Part One
The Changing Face of Evangelism

Part Two
The Home Bible Study

Part One

The Changing Face of Evangelism

Introduction

THIS IS NOT A BOOK written by a theologian. It is not written in a scholarly fashion, properly and rigorously cross-referenced with a full bibliography. It is not written in order to inform philosophers in ivory towers.

This book rather is written as a practical reflection of a practitioner of the gospel who has devoted his life to the work of sharing the gospel with a fallen world, and is still so engaged. My dearest wish is that all might see something of the loveliness of the Lord and come to fall in love with Him. There have been times when I have not been entirely sure that I am as skilled at sharing the gospel as I should be. I am certainly sure that as I look back, it was certainly true that there were long periods when I did not truly understand why my feeble efforts at sharing the gospel were not more successful than they appeared to be.

My reader is likely to be a Christian who is interested in sharing the gospel with others. This book is quite simply a gathering together of things which I now understand. These are things I have learned about sharing the gospel. Specifically this book is a statement that I wish someone had handed me more than thirty years ago when I first began to share my faith with others. It represents reflections on a lifetime of trying to share the gospel and things I have now come to believe about that process. During those thirty years, society here in Britain has been going through a major change, a revolution in how people react to the gospel message.

When I was growing up you heard people talk about how Great Britain was a Christian country. I am not sure any of us had a very clear picture of exactly what that meant. However it probably included some of the following thoughts:

- That the predominant religious background was Christian, albeit spread across a number of denominational traditions.

- That a substantial percentage of the population considered themselves to be members of a "Christian" denomination or church.

- That there were a large number of people who participated in Christian worship on a fairly regular basis.

- That, in schools, all children received some religious education or worship experience which was essentially Christian in nature.

- That the laws and principles on which the country operated were strongly influenced by Christian teachings or principles.

It is a long time since I heard anyone describe Great Britain as a Christian country. Commentators on today's society speak of a pluralistic society, with a rich diversity of backgrounds, ethnicity, religions and cultures. Indeed to suggest otherwise would be described as anachronistic and discriminatory. Society has changed.

On March 5th 2005, The Times carried a report blaming liberal and weak clergy for empty pews in British churches. A graph published in that report showed a decline in church attendance from around 1.6 million in 1968 to less than 1 million thirty years later. Researchers found "a widespread sense of anger and frustration" at what was happening to churches in the UK and Ireland. The 42-page report is an indictment of modern preaching and worship, illustrating how excessive liberalism and lack of conviction are driving worshippers from the pews.

Churches are being "silent" and "lukewarm" in the face of moral and social collapse, according to the £20,000, year-long study of 14,000 British churchgoers and those who have left the Church.

The report portrays a desire for sermons based on the Bible and traditional teaching, rather than on politics, social affairs or audience-pleasing stunts.

It calls for better apologetics, or Christian teaching, and claims that many clergy are unable to mount a convincing argument in defense of Christianity and are not interested in trying. When asked to explain why Christianity might be true, the common response is: "It is just a matter of faith."

The report says: "This has resulted in a growing number of people being left with the false impression that there are no strong reasons for Christian belief. Ultimately they abandon churchgoing and are mystified that Christianity continues to grow elsewhere in the world."

Researchers found that the thousands of people who still do go to church, do so out of a sense of duty and not because it brings them any fulfillment. They report widespread criticism of the current fashion for "family" or "all age" services which are bordering on entertainment rather than worship. One Shropshire churchgoer said: "I've seen balloons rising from the pulpit, fake moustaches and all manner of audience appeal but with no real message behind it."

The picture presented is one of declining membership and declining attendances. Generally the population is losing faith in a Christianity too bland to demand anything, and too wishy-washy to say anything significant about life or godliness.

The *Baptist Press* published an article on 14 January 2005 entitled *Apathy Replaces Religion in Britain.* In the article it indicated that a Gallup poll taken in 1968 said that 77% of the population said they believe in God. Today the figure is 44% according to the Telegraph in London. Amongst those who were not in the believers' camp, *The Telegraph's YouGov* poll said that most people seem to regard religion as a consumer commodity to be selected by those who happen to have a taste for it. Some 46% said they were agnostics and 35% claimed to be atheists whilst 18% said they did not know. Today, just 38% of Britons believe in heaven and 23% believe in hell.

In schools, whenever religion is mentioned, it is mentioned in the context of comparative religious studies where more time is devoted to non-Christian religions than to Christianity. It may be argued that the purpose of religious education is not to inculcate the principles and teachings of Christ but to help the population understand the diverse religious backgrounds of the multi-ethnic mix, which is modern Britain.

In some senses the same could be said of Western Europe. In February 2007 I read a mission report from France and a missionary there (I am grateful to Max Dauner who is currently involved in evangelistic work in Marseilles for the following information). It made a compelling point by telling this story.

He discussed a fascinating editorial in *The Daily Telegraph* (English Newspaper) concerning an interview given by Cardinal Ratzinger, the Prefect of the Sacred Congregation for the Doctrine of the Faith. (Note: since this time the cardinal has now been appointed Pope, and it will be interesting to see how his views may be modified by the perceived need of the Pope to build bridges towards Muslim and other faiths.) The cardinal sees Europe as a continent in the grip of a demographic and spiritual crisis. A falling birth-rate is 'altering the ethnic composition of Europe', as Muslim immigration transforms the ancient heartlands of Christendom. Churches are emptying as Christian culture is threatened by an, '*aggressive secularism, even an intolerant one*'.

This new secularism is no longer neutral, but hostile to public manifestations of Christianity, which is being marginalized and privatized. '*We must defend religious freedom against the imposition of an ideology that is being presented as if it were the only voice of rationality, whereas it is only the expression of a narrow rationalism.*'"

The incident that occasioned such anguish is the case of the conservative Italian Christian Democrat Rocco Buttiglione, who was declared unfit to serve as justice and home affairs commissioner by left-wing members of the European Parliament (MEPs): not for lack of competence, but for holding views that secular liberals find repugnant. He was asked whether, as a Catholic, he considered homosexuality a sin; he replied, as would most Catholics, that he did, but that this was in his view irrelevant to policy since it was not a crime; and that morality and law did not, and should not mix. He maintained that he also believed in freedom, which implied *"not imposing on others what one considers correct"*.

However this was not accepted by the MEPs. What followed would more correctly have been described as a witch-hunt. For Cardinal Ratzinger, the implication is that anybody who defends Christian orthodoxy is now excluded from public life. Buttiglione was forced to resign because of holding beliefs which one could describe as traditional Christian theology and morality. Buttiglione was seen as guilty of crass discrimination on the basis of sexual orientation which secular society sees as merely an alternative and equally acceptable life-style. Indeed to be seen as critical of homosexuality can be a dangerous position to hold. Dauner cites the example of a Protestant pastor in Sweden who was imprisoned for a month for preaching against it. Christianity has come full circle since the days of its persecution under the Roman Empire: an established Church no longer, it is now once again a persecuted band of the faithful. The editorial concludes with a call for ecumenical unity "for the sake of a united Christian front against secularism and jihad." (From the *Conservative Christian Fellowship* news site.)

Perhaps this illustrates the new secularism which dominates European culture. We can no longer assume when attempting to share the gospel that the current generation will have any knowledge of Christ or things Christian.

Recently friends from near Nashville, Tennessee told me a story that on first hearing I found difficult to believe. However because of my knowledge of these fine Christians I know that the story must be true.

In recent times, the film *The Passion of the Christ* was released. A congregation rented out a movie theatre and opened it up for a special showing for the congregation and as many friends as they could invite to attend. Many Christians did invite their friends to come along and view the movie hoping that it would stimulate discussion of what Christ had done for us by His death on the cross. One of the young girls brought along her friend. As the movie progressed towards its inevitable conclusion, the young visitor leaned over to her Christian friend and whispered, "They're not going to kill him are they?" It seems utterly stupefying that in Nashville Tennessee, on the buckle of the Bible belt, there might be young people who know so little about the story of Jesus that they might not know what happened to Him. Yet apparently this was so.

We have had one anecdote from France and mainland Europe, one from United States and we should also include one from the United Kingdom. A friend of mine was doing evangelistic work in Glasgow, the largest city in Scotland. One day he met a man who described himself as an "R.C." (i.e. Roman Catholic). The conversation carried on and at one stage the man said that he did not believe in God. My friend then interrupted with a call for explanation. "I thought you said you were a Roman Catholic, now you are saying you don't believe in God." The man was quick to reply, "that doesn't mean to say I can't be a good Catholic." The man did not attend religious services, did not contribute in any way to his church, did not believe in God but thought that he was still a good Catholic. Presumably this meant that he thought the Catholic church would bury him. What does it take to be a "good Catholic"? Is it a matter of faith, of life changing principles and morality, of a real and living hope that goes beyond this life and into eternity? Or is it something else… something merely to do with a family tradition, something to do with religious ceremonies that occur at notable times in one's life. For many the church is there for "hatches, matches and dispatches" and not a lot more. If these things are observed perhaps then this makes me a good catholic, or Christian of some kind.

Clearly this post Christian culture does make a huge difference to the way people think in our society. If that be so, what are the implications for evangelism in such a society?

What are some of the implications of this? First of all there are certain assumptions that must not be made.

We must **not** assume that…
1. people necessarily believe in the existence of God.
2. people necessarily believe that Jesus is the Son of God.
3. people are familiar with the teachings of Jesus.
4. their sense of morality is a Biblical one.

5. people are familiar with the things that Jesus did.

6. people are familiar with the teachings of the Bible.

7. people believe that the Bible is the inspired Word of God.

8. church attendance is seen as anything else other than a religious club for those who have a religious inclination.

Because some of us grew up in a world where we were introduced to the stories, actions, and teachings of Christ in public school and in Sunday School there is a tendency to assume some things which "ain't necessarily so." Not everyone is acquainted with the Jesus of the Bible. Not everyone has been exposed to Biblical teachings, miracles, parables or even morality. Secular people are essentially ignorant of all Biblical matters. In fact, it is interesting to watch what happens when an odd Biblical question comes up in a television quiz show. Almost invariably it goes unanswered. I had the experience of devising a little quiz to use in street evangelism in the city of Dundee, Scotland. My goal was to come up with questions which people in the street would know at least some of the correct answers to. We invited people to "Take the Bible challenge", with the promise that if they were prepared to take part, regardless of how many questions they got correct, we would give them a free Bible. After about ten redrafts, I finally came up with a set of eight questions which I thought would do the business. The problem was that the questions I thought were so simple just led to head scratching from the ordinary Dundonian. Some of the most basic questions concerning Christianity were completely beyond the secular man. Asking them to complete the phrase, "I am the Way, the Truth and _____". Most did not answer at all. Some put in the answer "light", with which I had some sympathy. But clearly this was a teaching with which they were not familiar. They had no idea who the apostle to the Gentiles was. Most seemed to know the name of the mother of Jesus. But beyond that there was almost zero knowledge of Biblical matters.

Our educational system is built on the premise of evolution and blind chance being the source of all things. We cannot assume that every person we meet will automatically believe in the existence of God. We may have to provide argument and present the case for faith.

Later in this work I will trace the development of my thought in this matter. I spent many years studying every book I could find to support the case for creation. Although I found all of that helpful to my own faith I am now no longer convinced that it is necessary to become the expert in Biological or Physical Science in order to support the case for the Scriptures. I will be describing a different approach later in this work.

In this pluralistic society, you are more likely to find people believing that Jesus was a good man who taught a good way of life, than believing that Jesus was the Word who became flesh and dwelt among us. Perhaps He was a prophet among many prophets who taught some good things and did some good. This is so clearly the antithesis of what Jesus said about Himself and His mission. However, we are not dealing with a society who knows what Jesus taught.

And though most Christians would affirm that they love the church, most secular people have a very negative view of the church. It may be a view which is mistaken. It is perhaps based on misconceptions, or on relations with some who are not the best example of what the church is supposed to be. Nevertheless the church is something which they do not harbor many positive opinions or feelings about. Jesus loved the church. We love the church. However, we cannot assume that secular man, wee Jimmy on the streets of Dundee, loves the church. For many people, their view of the church is colored by their experience of meeting judgmental attitudes, negative "vibes", religious condescension, and a seemingly anachronistic moral philosophy. (In writing this I am not saying the Biblical morality is dated... but as far as our post Christian society is concerned this is how they would view it.)

In order to truly help someone in counseling, it is essential that a non-judgmental attitude be shown towards the client. Even if I disapprove of what the person has been doing, yet I cannot influence or help that person unless I communicate that I am not there to condemn but to help them. I was once called in to do some marriage counseling with a couple I had never met before. In the course of the counseling session the wife told me with many tears that her husband raped her every night. I had a strong feeling of personal revulsion at such brutish behavior, yet I knew that if I said just what I felt like saying at that moment then the counseling session would be finished and my chances of making any difference in this dysfunctional relationship were gone. Rather I calmly asked him why he was doing that. He replied that he just wanted to show her how much he loved her. She sat on the chair weeping. I asked him to consider whether he thought this was working. Was she getting the message concerning this love? By the end of the session we had reached an agreement that for a period of one week he would desist from his nightly regime and his wife and I were able to convince him that this course of action would communicate love more effectively than his first plan. The next counseling session was in stark contrast. Rogers calls this unconditional positive regard. People cannot listen to you if they think you are there to condemn them. I am convinced that Jesus wants us to communicate concern and love even for the rapist. Not that we should communicate that we approve of their actions, but that we communicate that no matter what they have done Jesus loves them, and so do I. Many people have a very negative view of the church because they believe that the church, and Christians generally are judgmental towards them. Somewhere along the line we have failed to communicate the love of God as we ought.

Preachers in New Testament times majored on the death, burial and resurrection and we will need to do so.

Many of us virtually grew up on the miracles and parables of Jesus. The majority of people in society now have never heard them, never read them, and certainly never considered them. To read the New Testament with a non-Christian today means taking them into totally virgin territory. I will be returning to this thought later in this work also as it can be regarded as a disadvantage but perhaps in some ways we may learn to look at it as a blessing in disguise.

But from the observations above one thing is very clear. We cannot use a proof-text approach to evangelism in the present climate. Because a particular passage of Scripture tells us that we need to repent, or believe in Jesus, or be baptized is not sufficient. People need to be shown why this makes a difference. To prove that the Bible tells us we have to follow certain steps is insufficient unless we have established the right of the Bible to speak to us about these matters.

This again propelled me to launch into a study of proofs of the inspiration and inerrancy of the Bible, which was helpful to me and strengthened my faith. However now I conclude that we do not have to become an expert on proofs of inspiration in order to be effective in leading others to Christ. This will be expanded upon later.

Discussion Points

1. What signs can you see in your society that it might have entered into a post-Christian phase?

2. If Western culture has moved into a post Christian age, do we see this as an advantage or disadvantage for the church in its mission to share the gospel?

3. In what ways do we see this culture as a disadvantage for preaching the gospel?

4. In what ways may we consider it to be an advantage?

5. How does the post Christian world react to the vocabulary of Scripture and religious people?

6. How might this affect the ways in which the church tries to share the gospel with the world? Think in terms of the traditional ways in which the church seeks to share the gospel… gospel meetings, door knocking campaigns, special services, VBS, etc. How will these impact on a post Christian culture?

Chapter One

The Worldview Question

As we consider the matter of sharing the gospel with the world, we see that this presents us with a new challenge and calls for new strategies. How are we to share the message of hope and redemption with a world which thinks about religious things, thinks about morality and thinks about God in a wholly different way?

The world does not think about these things as the Christian thinks about them. The perspective is different. When the Christian converses with the world we find there is a language barrier that prevents real communication taking place. The language of the Christian world is different from the language of a naturalistic world in which God is excluded from the picture. We might say that each of us carries a model of the universe in our minds that tells us what the world is like and how we should live in it. How we view life, God, humanity, the universe and everything in it will be governed by our worldview.

The Marxist may interpret the world through economic frameworks, and see all human behavior as being shaped by economic and political factors. The Freudian sees the world through filters which interpret all human behavior as being rooted in sexuality and particularly in repressed sexual urges and instincts. The behavioralist sees all human behavior in terms of responses to certain stimuli. The Darwinian sees the world as a great cosmic accident resulting from natural selection and blind forces of nature and morality is only a matter of that which is beneficial to the survival of the species. The Christian views the world in quite a different way. We view the world in terms of a benevolent Designer and Builder, and man, made in the image of a moral God, making choices in keeping with His holy character.

It is clear that it does matter from which frame of reference we view the world. Newtonian Physics defined the world as following clearly defined principles of Physics (or laws of Physics). Einsteinian Physics said that these guidelines will be affected by our frame of reference. Are we making our measurements from a frame that is stationary or in motion? And that motion has to be regarded as relative to the body we are trying to observe or measure. Hence all observations and measurements are relative to our frame of reference. If we observe a dog running past us along the pavement, we might consider that the dog is moving very quickly. However if we view the same dog from the passenger seat of a speeding car, the dog appears to be moving slowly or even in reverse. It all depends on the frame of reference.

And so as we view the world from our own particular frame of reference. How we perceive the gospel will depend on our perspective. There can be little doubt that we live in a world in which Christian perspectives are rare. Our children are taught a different worldview in the school system from that which we read in Scripture. Evolutionary thought has permeated every field of endeavor and is popularized by full acceptance in education and in the media. And so we are busy teaching our children one worldview in the home or at church on Sunday, but society as a whole is presenting a more widely recognized worldview for the rest of the week. And even devoted Christians find themselves living with one worldview on Sundays but when they enter the world of business and work they are interfacing with a different worldview. The aura of worship dissipates after the glow of Sunday fades and we unconsciously end up absorbing the atheistic worldview which dominates in the world at large.

Which one is right? Which is true? The world says that your worldview might be true for you but not for me. And hence the Christian worldview is relegated to something which has a limited sense of truth associated with it. The world says that it is true in that it presents certain values which are held to be dear. This truth is subjective truth and should not be regarded in the same way as the objective truth that belongs to the science lab. Objective truth is seen as verifiable and repeatable. Objective truth is scientifically proven. Religious truth is seen as something that is subjectively true for you and leads to personal fulfillment. This truth is to do with personal values and is seen as a lesser kind of truth.

How you view the world depends on what you think the big picture truly is. The big picture is how I learn to interpret the world and my part in it. It allows me to contextualise myself and make sense of my existence. One of the reasons why we have such difficulty preaching the gospel today is that we are preaching to a population which has a totally different worldview from the Biblical one. Let us simply sketch out what I mean by thinking about our worldview in terms of a narrative. There are two very contrasting narratives that explain who you are, what you are doing here and where you are going.

Which is your story?

Let us think initially of a Biblical perspective. We might refer to this as a Christian worldview or narrative. And this is a story which sums up your world, and who you are, and the story of your existence. We might say that it is a story which involves five different phases.

- Creation
- Fall
- Redemption
- Sanctification
- Glorification.

This story defines your identity and your world.

Creation:

The modern fad of attempting to accept Jesus, and even the church but ditching the creation story strikes a blow at the very heart of the matter. The Bible begins with an eternally existent God who is the source of all things.

[1] In the beginning God created the heavens and the earth. Gen 1:1.

[1] In the beginning was the Word, and the Word was with God, and the Word was God. [2] He was in the beginning with God; [3] all things were made through him, and without him was not anything made that was made. Jn 1:1-3.

The Christian narrative begins with God. Notice how the Bible begins. In the beginning, God! And all things have God as the source, One who is eternal in the heavens. A heavenly designer who drew up His blueprint and made the world according to His plan.

My first degree was a Physics degree. And a Physicist in some senses can be thought of as someone who wants to make sense out of the Universe. The development of science would be impossible without assumptions. The first is that the universe is rational. If the universe did not have a rational structure, if different instrument readings at different times and places were simply random events which could not be brought into a coherent relation to each other, then science would be impossible. We could not speak of laws of Physics at all. Everything would be random, and wholly inexplicable.

I remember in one class being taught how to calculate the electrostatic force between two charged particles. The mathematical formula consisted of elements which included the charge on the two particles and the square of the distance between them. In another class I was taught how to calculate the gravitational force of attraction between two bodies. And the formula concerned the masses of the two bodies and the square of the distance between them. Indeed you could write down both equations side by side and they are identical in shape. The letters used for symbols for charge and mass are different but the symmetry of the two equations is quite remarkable. Why do these two fundamental forces of the universe look so similar? Why are the mathematical formulae identical in shape? If the universe is a random universe, which sprang accidentally from nothing, why is it that there is such symmetry? If the universe evolved by blind material forces acting randomly, why should it fit so neatly into mathematical formulae at all? Why does the math work? Why indeed should there be a law at all? Why is electrostatic attraction able to be calculated and predicted according to a law of Physics? If all is random then why should it even work the same way every time? Indeed when the truth is told by physical science we learn that there is a unique and delicate balance of forces which permits every atom in the universe to hang together and without this balance then there would not be a single cohesive atom in the universe, and no universe to observe. Where did such order and symmetry spring from? The symmetry and orderliness of physical laws testifies of the compelling logic of the Christian worldview.

I recall sitting in a meeting of the Institute of Physics in the University of Stirling, Scotland listening to one of the world's leading experimental experts speaking of his groundbreaking research into fundamental particles. There were certain things that had become clear from his research. It was clear that there was only a finite and small number of fundamental particles (a few more than we once thought, however a small finite number nonetheless). These particles could be split up into a very few families of particles (some of which only existing for nanoseconds). The researcher told us that they were now certain that they had identified all the fundamental particles which exist and there were no further fundamental particles to be found. He then went on to share the proof of this with us. The room was full of physicists. However, so advanced was the proof that few of us could understand it fully. He stated at the outset of his talk that he wanted to share with us the exciting new developments in fundamental particles. His lecture explained that there were only these very few types in existence and he posed the question, *why should this should be so*? I waited with baited breath for the explanation of why. I waited for over an hour as he explained with some intricacy the types of particles and their properties. And then when time was gone, he returned to the crux of the matter. Why? In a random universe, why are there not an infinite number of fundamental particles, evolving separately and randomly. Then the research physicist had to admit that he did not know why. Perhaps it might be postulated that at that point he had stepped out of his field of expertise. He was leaving the world of Physics and fundamental particles and entering the world of philosophy and worldview. The inescapable conclusion of the physics of fundamental particles is the existence of a Designer, whose masterpiece this universe is. The Christian worldview really does make sense.

Why only a few types of fundamental particles? If they arrived here accidentally and evolved in an accidental and random way, why should there not be an infinite variety of particles, so many we shall never discover them all or identify them all... and why not new types evolving all the time? All of his research fits perfectly with the Christian worldview. It does not fit with the Darwinian naturalistic worldview at all. These are elements which portray design and a Designer.

In the second year of my degree program we came to study the Second Law of Thermodynamics. As I sat in the lecture theatre waiting for the lecture to begin, the lecturer strode in and opened his lecture with these words, "Today we are going to study the Second Law of Thermodynamics and I will not entertain any discussion on the philosophical implications of the Second Law". I was totally mystified. What in the world was he talking about?

Just what is the Second Law and what could the philosophical implications be? I learned later that the basic thrust of the Second Law is that there is a trend in our Universe towards less and less order (greater entropy), and it is sometimes called the Law of Increasing Entropy. Put in its simplest form this law reflects that every process on earth is less than one hundred percent efficient and at the end of it there is always less energy available for any future process. Available energy is always decreasing. The philosophical implications are that this points back to some point in time in which there was maximum order, back to a time of maximum available energy, back to a time of creation. At creation the maximum order was put in place by an orderly God. And God's creation began with energy. And God said let there be light, and there was light. Evolution suggests that there should be increasing order in our universe. That the universe is continually ascending to higher and higher forms, more and more order. But this fundamental law of Physics says the very opposite. Which of the two worldviews is a better fit with our universe?

To anyone living in our society, you would think from the way that "truth" is presented, that creation is an illogical, unsupportable worldview whilst evolution is a scientific logic-based scenario. And yet from the few things we have considered it would appear that of the two the evolutionary, blind chance solution is the one that calls for the greater degree of faith. Design is as logical if not more logical than the cosmic accident hypothesis. And the reasons why evolutionary concepts are so much to the fore in education and in the media are a philosophical set of preconceptions rather than scientific. If we stand outside the evolution-based philosophical approach to worldview for a moment, its fragility becomes apparent. What could be more absurd as a philosophy than the idea that the whole universe came into existence by a very long series of highly improbable if not impossible accidents, and that it functions like a machine, constructed by nobody and for no purpose.

Christians commonly try to steer a compromise course. They seek to accept Jesus and fudge on Genesis. But accepting Jesus and rejecting Genesis is not really an option. They reject Genesis because they find themselves ill equipped to defend faith in creation. This compromise cannot work for it undermines God's big picture. The creation narrative defines who I am. And it is integral to the gospel narrative. To attempt to accept Jesus as Redeemer yet reject the story of Who made me, and in Whose image I am made, is self defeating. Can I really accept Jesus as the Word which became flesh and yet state that I am the product of blind chance and naturalistic forces? There is an underlying tension created that must lead to my being torn asunder. There are two pictures of me in this disunited story. But which is the real me? Can I be this split personality?

> [26] *Then God said, "Let us make man in our image, after our likeness; and let them have dominion over the fish of the sea, and over the birds of the air, and over the cattle, and over all the earth, and over every creeping thing that creeps upon the earth."* [27] *So God created man in his own image, in the image of God he created him; male and female he created them. Gen 1:26-27.*

The Christian narrative says that I am made in the image of a holy God. We are created in the image of a God that defines morality. Morality is defined in terms of His character. To be moral is to be like deity. And I am created in order to be like Him, made in His image. Thus I am more than the product of blind chance and natural selection. The principles which are involved in an evolutionary worldview must by definition be amoral. And in this view there can be no objective morality. Morality is that which assists me to survive and leave my gene legacy. But the Christian view is in sharp contrast to this. I am made to be like God. God is moral and defines morality. This says something about who I am, and the kind of being that I am. It separates me from the rest of creation, and sets me on a pedestal. God has made me. And humankind alone is created in His image. We are moral beings with moral choice. We are free moral agents to choose to do good or evil.

Creation defines where I have come from. It defines who I am. It defines where I am. And it defines where I am going. Hence in this creation narrative we can define origin, identity, location and objective.

We note that this story is linear. It is directional. There is a starting point and a finishing point. From this comes our sense of purpose. We are not here as some great accident of blind chance. But God made us and God put us here. He has not abandoned us here to form our own rules, our own morality and our own purpose. But He calls us to His purpose and defines morality in terms of His own character as an infinitely good God. He brings us purpose, direction and hence fulfillment because of who we are, created in His image. Life is a directional journey. And we define ourselves in terms of that journey.

Notice that there is a defining quality about the concept of creation. Creation defines my identity.

Evolution says that I am the craftiest of a wide diversity of animals, all of which arrived here by natural selection and survival of the fittest. This is who the Darwinist says I am. My purpose is to survive. My goal is to pass along my gene pool to a future generation and even after I have gone out of existence then I have a sense of continuing in some fashion. Even though at that time I will no longer be conscious of it, at least now I will have some sense of satisfaction that I will be continuing on.

Creation says I am made in the image of a Creator God who is a spiritual Being. And like my Creator, I have been made a spiritual being, an eternal soul that will go on after this physical existence has come to an end. My purpose is not survival or passing along my genes. My purpose is to live the way God intended that I should live, that I should experience the fullness of spiritual life in fellowship with my Creator. My purpose is to so live that I may continue to live in fellowship with Him in eternity and find my fullness in this life and in the next.

Fall:

The Biblical story is further defined by the events of Genesis chapter three. Then came the fall. Man rebelled against this heavenly perspective. God took the riskiest course of action, he created man with the ability to choose good or evil, to choose to follow Him or reject His ways and pursue wrong choices.

Each of us who are parents live with this scenario every day. This is what makes parenthood scary, and all the more so as we witness our children growing towards adulthood. No matter how much we would like to program our children into always making right choices we know that it cannot be done. For the child is growing up in the image of a God, who is a free moral agent, in a fallen world with all kinds of influences. We hope to influence our children to make right choices but deep down we know that we cannot make these choices for them. They must make their own choices.

Imagine two little boys who both want a puppy for Christmas. One little boy gets a wind-up puppy dog. It is good! It wags its tail and barks. It even does a back flip and lands on its feet again. The little boy can go across the room and point it in the direction of the far corner. If he runs to wait in the far corner it will eventually come to him and that brings a certain degree of satisfaction. The other little boy gets a real puppy. That little dog is a messy, noisy chewing machine, but one that runs up and licks your face. This puppy can be left in one corner and when the little boy goes to the other side of the room and calls it. There will be times when the puppy will actually come to this little boy and, tail wagging, jump up to lick his face. Which Christmas present do you think brought the greater joy?

The second one! The second one every time. Because the puppy chose to run to the little boy and offer devotion.

So also with God. God granted to us the risky gamble of free will. He could have made wind-up robots. But He didn't. He could have programmed us so that we could do nothing else but good. However that was not the kind of creation He wanted to make. He gave us the ability to choose. The end result of God's loving choice was that man made bad choices and fell. Man was given just the one rule, and he chose to break that one rule.

The result is that we live in a fallen world! And sometimes it is scary to live in this fallen world. And the imagination of man's heart seems to continually run after evil of every kind, and devising new ways of committing old sins. We have locks on our doors, immobilizers on our cars, pin numbers for our credit cards and a hundred other things because we live in a fallen world.

We are living with the consequences of bad choices made by man. This view of the world fits with our experience of the world. There is resonance between the Christian worldview and our experience of living in the world.

It is not that we inherit "sin" as some kind of genetic inheritance, some depraved DNA which is present because we are descended from fallen Adam. For sin is something that we do, and a sinful environment is the product of a fallen world. Scripture makes it plain that God will hold us responsible for the wrong choices *we* make not those of our forefathers.

> [20] *The soul that sins shall die. The son shall not suffer for the iniquity of the father, nor the father suffer for the iniquity of the son; the righteousness of the righteous shall be upon himself, and the wickedness of the wicked shall be upon himself. Ezek 18:20.*

Because we live in a world in which there are many people making wrong choices, then we are living with the consequences of sin. We may not have inherited the guilt of Adam's sin but we certainly have inherited the consequences of Adam's sin.

This again helps to define who we are. I am a person created in the image of God, with the freedom to choose between right and wrong. These definitions spread from the character of God my Creator.

Because of wrong choices I have made then I am a fallen man living in a fallen world. I ratified the bad choices of Adam my forefather. And as a result I live with the consequences of sin.

This says something about the nature of man. It says that man is a moral being because God is a moral being. It says that we are free moral agents, with a God given ability to choose right or wrong, and indeed that we even have an innate sense of right and wrong. Listen to how people speak around you... "You should given me a bit of your chocolate, I gave you a piece of mine." As human beings we have a very strong sense of right and wrong. Some years ago I remember listening to an item on the evening news. A tragic accident had happened to the brother of a very famous politician. The man was a farmer and he had been killed on his farm by being trampled by a cow. I do not wish to trivialize the seriousness of this accident or minimize the effect of the loss on the man's family. This is no joke. It was however noticeable that the news story did not go on to say that the cow had been arrested and was soon to be brought up in court and tried for culpable homicide. It was not reported even that the cow had been destroyed. If a man had done this, we would expect something of this nature to be included in the news item. However not when it was a cow. Why? We accept that a man should be held accountable for his actions. Man is a moral being and makes moral choices and as a result should be called upon to answer for the choices that he makes. Not so with the cow! We all accept in our heart of hearts that we are moral beings making moral choices. And deep down we accept that we should be held accountable for our moral decisions.

We go to the pond to feed the ducks and see a smaller duck than all the others. The evolutionary worldview says survival of the fittest. Evolutionary theory says that only the strongest should survive. However something inside of us says this is wrong! We go out of our way to make sure that our hunks of bread fall to the weak duck and try to support that life. We have this sense of morality, an idea that some things are right and other things are wrong. These things are often the very opposite of survival of the fittest.

And some of the most dear doctrines of the present age are fundamentally at odds with the Darwinian worldview. You cannot fail to have noticed much discussion in recent years about biodiversity. It is perceived that it is a right and good thing to preserve species and not let certain species die out. But many species are no longer with us. And indeed, if it is all a matter of survival of the fittest why should any species which is struggling be supported? Let it die off and be gone and let the rest of the animal kingdom divide up the spoils accordingly. And if that species be Homo sapiens then so be it.

Darwinian worldview should lead us to be interested only in our own survival, and leave the rest to fend for themselves. Yet there is something in us which rebels at this. It is right to save the endangered species. It is a good thing! Under whose definition is it right and good? What makes it right and good? The Christian worldview states it very simply. We are created by God and given dominion over the world in which He has made, to look after it, to manage it. We as the pinnacle of God's creation are created as the climax of God's creative work and as such are created with a responsibility to care for God's creation. He made us as stewards of this world! It is right and good that we should exercise care and protection over endangered species, and feed the little duck whenever we can. This resonates with the Christian worldview. This inner sense of responsibility and right and wrong shouts the amen to the Christian worldview. But it does not fit at all well with the Darwinian worldview.

Similarly think of the recent popularity of all matters ecological. There is a strong lobby for "green" thinking and policy-making. And it seems that every political party is falling over itself to appear more green in the eyes of the electorate. Why? It is because there is a very prevalent belief that we should take care of this world in which we live and protect it from harm. Some things are just right and some things are just wrong! If I am created by God and given dominion over this world to exercise care for it, this resonates with the feelings we have inside ourselves, and ecology and biodiversity make perfect sense, at least from a Christian worldview. As Newbigin put it:

> "The only way to seek the integrity of creation is in a
> recovery of the sense of responsibility to the Creator and in a

recognition that we have to answer before his judgment seat for the way we have exercised the stewardship he entrusted to us".[1]

As we shall see when we examine the other worldview, worldly man says there is no such thing as sin. There is no right and there is no wrong. The only right is that which demonstrates itself to be supportive of the survival of this accidental assemblage of molecules which I like to define as me. I will choose whatever I have the opportunity of choosing which may support self satisfaction, fulfillment or survival and this is the only right there is.

The Bible screams no... you are more than this. You are the pinnacle of God's creation, made in His very image. You are created with choice. You may choose to do that which is right or you may choose otherwise. But there are consequences of our choices. The fall is a reality. We fall out of relationship with the God who made us. We lose our innocence in acts of rebellion against a loving God. And the result is that we find ourselves cut off from the person we were designed to be and there is a sense of dissatisfaction deep in our souls because we are not living the life we were designed for, and called to, by a loving Creator God. And so for a great many people, we live with a sense of disjunction. I was meant for higher and better things. The wise man Solomon in his musings and experimenting with philosophies (the book of Ecclesiastes) takes a stab at expressing this under the direction of the Holy Spirit:

> [10] *I have seen the business that God has given to the sons of men to be busy with.* [11] *He has made everything beautiful in its time; also he has put eternity into man's mind, yet so that he cannot find out what God has done from the beginning to the end. Eccles 3:10-11.*

God has put a sense of eternity into man's mind. No wonder. We are created by an eternal God. It would be surprising if this were not the case. Animals may fight against extinction. But man has an

---

[1] From "A Word in Season: Perspectives on Christian World Missions" by Lesslie Newbigin, published by Saint Andrew Press (1994), p144.

innate sense of eternity, and an innate sense that we were created for eternity.

Fallen man may be brought to realize his plight… and grasp the grace of God when it is extended to him. This is a Christian worldview. And it is why we preach the gospel. And it is why men accept the gospel.

But some men will reject the gospel if they cannot see their predicament. If they do not accept that they have fallen, why should they grasp the lifeline lowered to them by a gracious God. The lifeline seems incongruous and unnecessary. It may be necessary if you have a deluded religious worldview, but personally I don't accept your ideas of absolute morality, guilt and the need for redemption. Hence the naturalistic-worldview-man looks at the gospel through different eyes and wonders at this strange beast, the religious man, who goes into great raptures over the greatness of the gospel. The naturalistic-worldview-man regards the gospel as about as necessary as a bicycle for a haddock. If you reject the existence of sin, the reality of right or wrong, then there can be no such thing as the fall. Since man refuses to accept that he has fallen, there is no sense of need or predicament. Secular man has no real concept of redemption.

Redemption:

"I've been redeemed, by the blood of the Lamb", sings the Christian in a rapturous outpouring of thanksgiving. The naturalistic worldview man stands by in amazement. To him this is complete gobbledygook. If there is no fall, there is certainly no need for redemption. And if the fall is illusory, then so is the redemption. Little wonder that worldly man finds the good news of redemption to be an irrelevance. If I deny the reality of the fall, then I must deny the relevance of redemption. It becomes merely a religious myth, which seems to help some people in the evolution of their value system. "I once was lost but now I'm found!" "Good for you… personally I was never lost" croons the evolutionary-worldview-man.

But for the Christian the story of redemption is the narrative which defines who we are. We are the redeemed of God! Just as Israel in the Old Testament was redeemed from slavery in Egypt, so we also are redeemed from the slavery of sin.

> *[16] Do you not know that if you yield yourselves to any one*
> *as obedient slaves, you are slaves of the one whom you obey,*
> *either of sin, which leads to death, or of obedience, which*
> *leads to righteousness? [17] But thanks be to God, that you who*
> *were once slaves of sin have become obedient from the heart*
> *to the standard of teaching to which you were committed,*
> *[18] and, having been set free from sin, have become slaves of*
> *righteousness. Rom 6:16-18.*

As Israel of old was a redeemed people, freed from slavery in Egypt, so is the *new Israel* of God today a redeemed people. We are set free from slavery to sin and set on a pilgrimage to the promised land of heaven. And down through the ages, Israel was taught to be thankful for their redemption through the system of worship referred to as the Passover. And now we are taught thankfulness through our Passover Lamb, Jesus, who was slain for our redemption, and by His blood we are set free.

Part of our identity is that we view ourselves as a redeemed people. Once we were no particular people, but now we have a sense of identity with the people of God, a new spiritual nation.

> *[9] But you are a chosen race, a royal priesthood, a holy nation,*
> *God's own people, that you may declare the wonderful deeds*
> *of him who called you out of darkness into his marvelous*
> *light. [10] Once you were no people but now you are God's*
> *people; once you had not received mercy but now you have*
> *received mercy.   1 Pet 2:9-10.*

When the Christian thinks about who he is, he thinks of the Passover Lamb, and the new redeemed people of God, freed from the slavery of sin, free from the bondage of a hard taskmaster, in order to be the willing servant of a loving Leader and Shepherd. This is who I am!

And no wonder this worldview sets us apart from the naturalistic evolutionary worldview. There is no sense of identity there! There is no sense of redemption. There is no sense of thankfulness for what God has done and is doing for us and with us.

Sanctification:

Sanctification is the story of the Christian life. Jesus accepts me "just as I am", but loves me too much to leave me in that condition and the story of the Christian life is the story of change. It is God at work in our lives to make us more like the Savior. At our baptism we receive the gift of the Indwelling Spirit of God. And the Spirit is at work in us to bring us to higher levels of spirituality, displaying more of the fruit of the Spirit day by day.

> *[18] And we all, with unveiled face, beholding the glory of the Lord, are being changed into his likeness from one degree of glory to another; for this comes from the Lord who is the Spirit. 2 Cor 3:18.*

And what difference does this make to our identity?

It inserts purpose and direction into our lives. Life is not an endless cycle of meaningless events and transitory relationships. Up one minute and down the next. It is not some pointless existence which is going nowhere and means nothing. Rather life is filled with a holy purpose and a heavenly direction. We are in the process of being beautified by the Spirit of God to enable us to become like Jesus. This is a narrative which summarizes what your life are about. And the point is that your life is about something, it is not about nothing.

For the naturalistic man, the only purpose in life is to seek fulfillment through pleasure. Fill your life with pleasure and there you will find fulfillment. But Scripture, history and personal experience give the lie to this philosophy.

Peterson in his excellent version *The Message* renders Solomon's take on this from Ecclesiastes chapter two:

> *Oh I did great things:*
> *Built houses,*
> *Planted vineyards,*
> *Designed gardens and parks*
> *And planted a variety of fruit trees in them,*
> *Made pools of water*
> *To irrigate the groves of trees.*

I bought slaves, male and female,
Who had children, giving me even more slaves;
Then I acquired large herds and flocks,
Larger than any before me in Jerusalem.
I piled up silver and gold, loot from kings and kingdoms.
I gathered a chorus of singers to entertain me with song,
And – most exquisite of all pleasures –
Voluptuous maidens for my bed.
Oh how I prospered! I left all my predecessors in Jerusalem
far behind, left them behind in the dust. What's more, I kept
a clear head through it all. Everything I wanted I took – I
never said no to myself, I gave in to every impulse, held back
nothing. I sucked the marrow of pleasure out of every task
– my reward to myself for a hard day's work! Then I took a
good look at everything I'd done, looked at all the sweat and
hard work. But when I looked, I saw nothing but smoke.
Smoke and spitting into the wind. There was nothing to any
of it. Nothing.

Solomon's description of worldly man's life view is immediately relevant because it is just as modern as the day when he wrote it. This pleasure seeking philosophy is at the last unfulfilling. It does not bring the satisfaction that man imagines it might.

All of this is in complete contrast to the Christian worldview and its five stages of narrative we noted earlier. We as Christians need to appreciate what a huge difference has been accomplished in our lives because of this new narrative. We derive our whole sense of identity, purpose and being out of this big picture. We thrill at the realization that God's big picture of the universe has a special place and a special role for us. This is who we are. Look! You see it. There you are in God's picture! And your life makes a difference in the eyes of God. In this you find yourself. And consequently, in this you find your fulfillment.

[1] See what love the Father has given us, that we should
be called children of God; and so we are. The reason why
the world does not know us is that it did not know him. [2]
Beloved, we are God's children now; it does not yet appear

29

what we shall be, but we know that when he appears we shall be like him, for we shall see him as he is. ³ And every one who thus hopes in him purifies himself as he is pure. 1 Jn 3:1-3.

The greatest thrill of our lives is that God loved us enough to adopt us and we can be called the children of God. And because we are His children He is in the process of protecting us, sustaining us, feeding us, guiding us, and preparing us for a home in heaven. Wonder of wonders, joy of joys, this is who you are. And the only way you can apprehend this is to catch a glimpse of God's big picture for you, His holy narrative for you.

The naturalistic man's worldview is in stark contrast to this. Life is not directional it is cyclical. We pass through various cycles heading nowhere. There is no great purpose undergirding our existence. In a Darwinian view I cannot look at my life and ask where I am going and how far I have come. My life has no purpose. It has no goal other than survival. As a result, my life is doomed to failure for all organisms must of necessity die and go out of existence. There is no place for optimism or positivism. My only purpose is to survive and I won't.

Each of us has to decide which of these two worldviews makes the most sense to us and which of them we wish to define our lives. What does your inner voice say to you? Are you a pointless person, with no purpose, no direction, no hope and no goal? Or do you sense that you are much more than this? Which of the two worldviews helps you to understand yourself and your world?

Glorification:

The final stage in the Christian worldview is the passage from this life into glory. Some might say that the point of the pilgrimage of Israel through the wilderness was that one day they might cross the Jordan River and take possession of the land of promise. "On Jordan's stormy banks I stand and cast a wishful eye, to Canaan's fair and happy land where my possessions lie". When we sing that song, what are we singing about? Is it a song about ancient Israel under the leadership of Moses or Joshua? No it is not! It is a song about our pilgrimage and how one day we shall cross over the flooded waters of the Jordan (spiritually) into our heavenly promised land. Death's cold chill from the waters of the Jordan shall not discourage us nor diminish our sense of expectancy. For one day we shall cross over and take possession.

And the message of the gospel is one of hope.

> [1] *"Let not your hearts be troubled; believe in God, believe also in me.* [2] *In my Father's house are many rooms; if it were not so, would I have told you that I go to prepare a place for you?* [3] *And when I go and prepare a place for you, I will come again and will take you to myself, that where I am you may be also. Jn 14:1-3.*

> [3] *Blessed be the God and Father of our Lord Jesus Christ! By his great mercy we have been born anew to a living hope through the resurrection of Jesus Christ from the dead,* [4] *and to an inheritance which is imperishable, undefiled, and unfading, kept in heaven for you,* [5] *who by God's power are guarded through faith for a salvation ready to be revealed in the last time. 1 Pet 1:3-5.*

Atheists may mock and talk about pie in the sky when you die. But I think it preferable to extinction and redistribution of our molecules in the muck of a godless, meaningless, directionless universe. Because the Christian hope is wonderful does not mean that it is not true!

And we get a sense of proportion about life, about riches, about suffering, about pain, about pleasure, about people, about God, about morality and about just about everything else from this narrative which includes the hope of heaven.

Now that is what we call a big picture! That is some kind of narrative! But what is the alternative? Let us look at the alternative and compare it in terms of how it explains this universe, life, morality and meaning.

Christian Worldview	**Evolutionary Worldview**
Creation	Blind chance evolution
Fall	Accidental assemblage of molecules which is me
Redemption	Extinction- disassembling of molecules
Sanctification	evolution goes on without me
Glorification	nothingness

It would be difficult to imagine a starker contrast than this. The stark nihilism of the Darwinian naturalistic worldview would crush the most intrepid human spirit. You are not created in the image of God, you are a moderately smart animal. You have no inner you at all, just an assemblage of neurons and electrical impulses. There is no morality. There is no direction for the evolutionary worldview is cyclical, not directional. It may be claimed to be directional but if it is, it is directional without me. I end by extinction and the process goes on without me, though my molecules may get reused in some way. This narrative is already making me feel depressed just by writing these words down.

- Who am I? - an unplanned accident.
- Where am I going? - I am headed for extinction.
- Why am I here? – No reason.
- Who cares? - Well, essentially, nobody cares.

Now doesn't that sound attractive as a philosophy for life?

The Christian worldview is not wrong because it is filled with hope and wonder. The evolutionary worldview is not automatically right because it is filled with demeaning despair and nothingness. One of them is correct. Both cannot be right. One of them is correct and the other is wrong! And how we decide which is correct is where we are going with this book.

How can we know? And if we can know how do we communicate with a world which is increasingly dedicated to a diametrically opposed worldview?

Gospel Sharing;

As we study the Book of Acts, we see some of the "gospel sharing" that was done in New Testament times. Perhaps some might have expected them to major in areas which are barely mentioned if at all.

1. We might have expected them to major on the change in covenants between the old covenant established on Sinai between God and Israel and the new covenant of Christ established with all mankind on Golgotha. This is dealt with in some detail in the epistles, but with reference to gospel preaching in Acts, it hardly gets a look in.

2. We might perhaps expect some mention of the changeover from the synagogue to the church. It is not mentioned.

3. We might expect some discussion of the changeover from Old Testament worship (sacrifices, the role of the priests etc) and New Testament worship. We have to wait to study the Book of Hebrews before this is dealt with in any detail. It is not there in the early gospel sharing.

However, gospel sharing centers on one thing.

It is not a study of covenants, or systems of worship, or organizational matters concerning the New Covenant, as important as these things might be considered to be.

Gospel sharing is about a person. And if we are smart we will realize that gospel sharing in the 21st century is still about a person. Essentially people need to be introduced to Jesus.

We are dealing with a population who are ignorant of Jesus. This statement is not meant to be an insult. It is a succinct statement of fact. They know not Jesus. Our task is the same as that of Philip when he spoke with the Ethiopian in Acts chapter 8. *And beginning with the same Scripture he told him the good news of Jesus.*

And how are those who are immersed in the evolutionary worldview ever to catch a glimpse of the glory of this big picture? It will be done by catching something of the majesty of the Master. It will be in coming to know Jesus that we get our big picture brought into focus. The narrative of our lives can only become clear to us as we get to know Jesus. And the biggest challenge facing the church today is to present Jesus to the world.

And so our discussion thus far has focused our attention on the difference between two contrasting worldviews. And perhaps we might be tempted to think that the key to everything then is to subject everyone we wish to reach to a few lessons on worldview… if people could understand the stark choice, then they would surely select the Christian worldview as the correct one and the attractive one.

However would an educational program, sorting out the worldview crisis be a successful way of sharing the gospel in a post Christian culture? The answer is probably not. What will be successful is to point people to Jesus. It will still be the power of the good news about Jesus, which will help others to put their story into perspective. It will still be the cross at the center of the picture that makes sense of the big picture in every individual's life.

Chapter Two

The Beginning Point of Gospel Preaching

1. Right Internal Conditions:

- Convinced we have something worth sharing.
- Deep appreciation for the grace of God.
- Deep appreciation for the sacrifice of Christ.
- Deep appreciation for the church to which we have been added.

One feature of modern day churches is that there are few who are engaged in the process of sharing the gospel. This is the principal reason why some churches are not growing. Growing churches have a number of individuals who are engaged in evangelistic activity. Dying churches are those who leave evangelism to the preacher or perhaps just one or two activists.

The gospel is still powerful. It is still God's dynamic power to save men and women. It still convicts and convinces. It still transforms and inspires people today. However the church is not sharing the gospel message as it should. One mistake that the church often makes is that it sees the work of evangelism as the work of an evangelist. And yet the Scripture makes it clear that the work of the evangelist is to take the lead in evangelism, train others in evangelism and equip the church to evangelize.

For this to happen we as individual Christians have to have the right internal conditions. There must be a deep conviction that we have the right Father who loves us, the right Savior who died for us, and we have been added by God to His church, the right church on earth. We have to be convinced that we have the right big picture and we passionately want others to see the greatness of this vision.

When we have a proper grasp of it, nothing could be more astounding than the grace of God. And I mean by that the grace of God towards me. When we think of the great hymns of the church, there is within them a sense of wonder at the grace of God. There is astonishment at the love and mercy of our Father in heaven. And yet there are times when we have to wonder where this astonishment has gone in the church. We have to marvel with John Newton…

> Amazing grace, how sweet the sound,
> That saved a wretch like me
> I once was lost but now am found,
> Was blind but now I see.

This has to be my song. I have to marvel at it, and major in extolling the benefits and beauties of the manifold grace of God. All other pastimes and interests, hobbies, patriotism, nepotism and any other kind of "ism" pale to insignificance before the grace of God towards me.

Philip Yancey tells a great story in his book[2]. Jessye Norman was an African-American singer called upon to perform at a charity concert in Wembley Stadium, England. Many performers had gathered together for this performance though mostly they were raucous rock bands. And clearly that is what the audience had come for. This rock concert was to celebrate the changes being wrought in South Africa at that time, as it came out of Apartheid. Finally the time came and Jessye Norman strode onto the stage alone. There was no back up band, no drums, no synthesizer, just a lone figure in a flowing African gown. She

---

[2] "What's So Amazing About Grace?" by Philip Yancey, published by Zondervan.

was illuminated by a lone spotlight. She opened her mouth and began to sing. The a *capella* song she began to sing to that rowdy crowd was John Newton's, *Amazing Grace*. By the end of the first verse the crowd had quietened down. Seventy thousand rock fans fell silent. By the end of the second verse the soprano had the crowd in the palm of her hand. By the time she reached the third verse, strangely a number in the crowd had begun to join in, searching back in the depths of their memories for words they had long ago forgotten. Jessye Norman later said that she had no idea what power was at work in Wembley stadium that night except that perhaps the world hungers for that grace which only God supplies.

There is a world of people out there who have been taught a falsehood. They have been indoctrinated with a worldview which leaves them hopeless and helpless. Even if they are not conscious of it and could not vocalize it nor explain it… they are crying out for hope and meaning.

If everything in your education and learning has conspired to teach you that your life is a meaningless nothing, then it colors how you look at the world and everything in it. Think of the impact this has on your moral framework. Why do good? Why refrain from doing bad? Think of how this impacts your view of society. Society becomes your competition for biological survival. Think about how this impacts your sense of identity. Who are you really? Some little pointless organism competing for survival with millions of others. Where are you going? Nowhere! Why are you here? No reason! What is the end of your existence? Pointless extinction at the end of a pointless life!

But if you are in Christ, that grace is yours. When we are truly convinced that we have something worth sharing, we share it. Suppose we have found the best washing powder we have ever bought. It cleans the clothes at all temperatures. It is good on synthetics and it is good on natural fibers. It takes out stains that all other powders leave behind. Would you tell your neighbor about it? Suppose you have just learned that one car dealership in town will give you twice what your car is worth in trade in. Would you talk to your friends about it and share that advantageous knowledge with them?

The answer is that when we are truly convinced that we have something of great value we can't stop talking about it to anyone who will listen.

When we have a proper appreciation for the grace of God, for the love of Christ and for the supreme value of the fellowship of the Holy Spirit and His church, then nothing will persuade us to be silent.

If all of that is so, then we will not require to be urged to share our faith with others, we will want to do that automatically.

2. Scratching where people itch:

What are the senses of need that people have? Sometimes we are offering to scratch where people don't itch. How would you react to that in a physical sense? You would find such offers an irritation. For example, suppose we took out a TV advertising campaign offering to teach people the order of the kings in the divided kingdom. How many people would respond to such a campaign? No doubt there might be the odd person, but there would not be many. And that person would probably be an odd person. This is because this is not what people perceive themselves as needing. So also, if our thrust is an alternative worship style, an alternative church organizational structure... etc etc. We have to be sure that we are offering something that people believe they need. Paul Little[3] makes a list of what itches man:

a. Purposelessness. i.e. some people are wondering about the apparent pointlessness of life. What am I doing here? What is life? Where am I going? What is it all about? And no one seems to have appropriate answers to these serious questions.

> [12] *Again Jesus spoke to them, saying, "I am the light of the world; he who follows me will not walk in darkness, but will have the light of life." Jn 8:12*

b. Fear of death. Most people have a fear of death. It is seen as the great unknown. People make the statement, "no one has been there

---

[3] *How to Give Away Your Faith* by Paul E. Little published by IVP

and come back to tell us what it is like." And yet in the last analysis, for the Christian, that statement is untrue. We do have someone who has been there and come back, and does tell us what it is like. The world craves such certainty about death.

> *[14] Since therefore the children share in flesh and blood, he himself likewise partook of the same nature, that through death he might destroy him who has the power of death, that is, the devil, [15] and deliver all those who through fear of death were subject to lifelong bondage.   Heb 2:14-15.*

> *[25] Jesus said to her, "I am the resurrection and the life; he who believes in me, though he die, yet shall he live, [26] and whoever lives and believes in me shall never die. Do you believe this?" Jn 11:25-26.*

And we would go further than that. There is an innate sense in man that we were not created for such temporary existence. There is a sense in which we crave what we were designed for… eternal existence with God.

c. Desire for inner peace. When man is separated from his creator, and not living the kind of life that our Maker determined that he should live, it leads to inner conflict. He is beset by doubts and questionings all the time. He also wonders about whether he is following the right course, doing the right thing, being the right kind of "me". It is the opposite of certainty. Is there a God? Are we truly made in the image of God? Does this God care about me? And yet God does not wish us to live in this kind of quandary all the time.

> *[6] Have no anxiety about anything, but in everything by prayer and supplication with thanksgiving let your requests be made known to God. [7] And the peace of God, which passes all understanding, will keep your hearts and your minds in Christ Jesus. Phil 4:6-7.*

> *[27] Peace I leave with you; my peace I give to you; not as the world gives do I give to you. Let not your hearts be troubled, neither let them be afraid. Jn 14:27.*

d. Loneliness. When you think of the most daunting days of your life…. First day at school, first day at high school, going into hospital etc etc. What makes these experiences more daunting than anything else is the prospect that we might have to face these alone? And yet Christians walked bravely into the arena and gave their lives in utter confidence. Daniel walked fearlessly into the den of lions. Shadrach, Meschack and Abednego bravely marched into the fiery furnace. David walked into battle with the giant Goliath. And all of these things were possible because they realized that they were not alone.

> *[19] Go therefore and make disciples of all nations, baptizing them in the name of the Father and of the Son and of the Holy Spirit, [20] teaching them to observe all that I have commanded you; and lo, I am with you always, to the close of the age." Mt 28:20.*

> *[5] Keep your life free from love of money, and be content with what you have; for he has said, "I will never fail you nor forsake you." [6] Hence we can confidently say, "The Lord is my helper, I will not be afraid; what can man do to me?" Heb 13:5.*

In fact Christianity is all about relationship. Some writers have called this Relational Theology. For in becoming a Christian we are in the business of establishing and maintaining right relationships in every aspect of our lives. If becoming a Christian means anything it is certainly about establishing a right relationship with God. And this right relationship with the God who made us is what brings stability and sense into our existence. We cannot live fulfilled lives whilst out of sorts with the God who made us. Christianity brings us into a right relationship with God, and reconciliation becomes a reality. It also establishes a sense of resonance with our inmost selves. We make peace with ourselves. This is because there is a new harmony created between what we were created to be and what we have now become. We are at peace. Paul calls this the *peace which passes all understanding*. This also produces a new relationship with others, a relationship not based on self-seeking and pleasure, but we are freed to seek the good of others confident in what God has promised us. If a creation-based worldview gives us a high view of ourselves, it also gives us a high view of others. They are also created in the image of God, and God cares for them as much as He cares for us. This becomes the basis for right relationships on a horizontal plane. In fact only right relationships in the vertical plane establish the foundation of right relationships horizontally.

e. Lack of self-control (guilt) If I am honest with myself, then I know that there are times when I disappoint myself. And most of us are well aware that there are times when we know that we do not behave as we ought, do not speak as we ought, and do not think as we ought. We know that there are times when we are a disappointment to others but also a disappointment to ourselves. We know that we have lacked self-control and done things that we shouldn't. It is a foolish man indeed who does not see these things concerning himself. Then perhaps we promise ourselves that we will change and not be like that. But efforts to change are not met with great success. This actually highlights two problems which are usually rolled together into one in the minds of the majority. The two problems are…

> i) The power of sin which corrupt us
> ii) The guilt of sin which cripples us

In Christ we have the answer to both problems.

> *[17] But thanks be to God, that you who were once slaves of sin have become obedient from the heart to the standard of teaching to which you were committed, [18] and, having been set free from sin, have become slaves of righteousness. [19] I am speaking in human terms, because of your natural limitations. For just as you once yielded your members to impurity and to greater and greater iniquity, so now yield your members to righteousness for sanctification. Rom 6:17-19.*

Husbands, love your wives, as Christ loved the church and gave himself up for her, [26] that he might sanctify her, having cleansed her by the washing of water with the word, [27] that he might present the church to himself in splendor, without spot or wrinkle or any such thing, that she might be holy and without blemish.   Eph 5:25-27.

[14] And he said, 'The God of our fathers appointed you to know his will, to see the Just One and to hear a voice from his mouth; [15] for you will be a witness for him to all men of what you have seen and heard. [16] And now why do you wait? Rise and be baptized, and wash away your sins, calling on his name.' Acts 22:14-16.

Perhaps there has been a tendency to try to market the church as a religious social club. We compete with other such clubs to see who has the most vibrant worship services, or the best children's organizations, or the most dynamic preacher, or the most attractive décor. And yet if truth be told, all of these things are incidental. ***It is not the church's role to compete with other churches. It is the church's role to preach the gospel and bring the lost to Jesus.***

When we look at this analysis it is amazing how closely the Christian worldview answers each point and satisfies it completely.

The Darwinian worldview says that life is purposeless. It is futile. But the Christian worldview cries out that we do have a purpose. Our purpose is to glorify God, by the fruit of our lips and the fruit of our lives. In fulfilling that purpose we find a richness that the world cannot match. My purpose is to put on the divine nature, to be changed into the likeness of the Savior and in so doing I become what my great Maker and Designer intended me to be and hence find a sense of completion and fulness.

The Darwinian worldview says that death is the end, it is going out of existence and hence death is the ultimate object of fear. And so some people spend their whole lives with the fear of death as a sword of Damocles hanging above their heads. The writer to the Hebrews calls this a bondage, *through fear of death subject to a lifelong bondage.* And yet in Christ, the Christian worldview offers freedom from this bondage. In Christ we have assurances that this life is not all there is. That death is not the end. It is the beginning of a new and wonderful phase of our existence.

> *[25] Jesus said to her, "I am the resurrection and the life; he who believes in me, though he die, yet shall he live, [26] and whoever lives and believes in me shall never die. Do you believe this?" Jn 11:25-26.*

> *[1] "Let not your hearts be troubled; believe in God, believe also in me. [2] In my Father's house are many rooms; if it were not so, would I have told you that I go to prepare a place for you? [3] And when I go and prepare a place for you, I will come again and will take you to myself, that where I am you may be also. Jn 14:1-3.*

The Darwinian worldview offers no peace. Christ offers the peace that passes all understanding.

The Darwinian worldview does not answer the basic loneliness in a man's soul. The evolutionist says that man is alone in the universe. Man is the pinnacle of the great evolutionary accident and there is no other power and no other source. Man in his innermost spirit may long for fellowship with the eternal One but there is no such being. But for the Christian, it is in the relationship with God that we find our truest companion.

> *[3] And this is eternal life, that they know thee the only true God, and Jesus Christ whom thou hast sent. Jn 17:3.*

> *[23] Jesus answered him, "If a man loves me, he will keep my word, and my Father will love him, and we will come to him and make our home with him. Jn 14:23.*

The Darwinian regards guilt to be a complex to be treated and healed. And an excessive sense of guilt can be enormously destructive. However a total absence of guilt can be just as serious and just as destructive. In the human body we want to immediately treat pain.

We spend huge amounts of money buying over the counter pain medication. But when our bodies malfunction and do not send pain messages this can be very problematic. If your hand will not send normal pain messages to the brain then you may put your hand in the fire without realizing it and hence suffer worse damage. Guilt is like that. The Darwinian says that ultimately there is no right and wrong and hence there can be no guilt. If you feel guilt then it is a complex to be treated. And the solution? Sweep it under the carpet and learn to ignore it. This leads to grave psychological problems. The guilt does not truly go away but lies dormant.

Only the Christian worldview deals with this need in a constructive way. In Christ we do not sweep guilt under the carpet but we bring it out into the full glare of the light… and we find our complete forgiveness and the expunging of guilt utterly and fully. As far as the east is from the west, so far does He remove our guilt from us.

3. Interacting with the World:

So how do we interact with the world out there? We have thought about what the burning issues for mankind are. We have thought about the fact that we consider ourselves to be greatly blessed and people who have something to share. So now where do we start?

Well the first phase is when we reach out and find someone to speak to about what God has done for us and wants to do for them.

Can we think of ways in which we as an individual or as a church try to begin this process of reaching out with the gospel? How do we do it? Some of the most common ways are perhaps the following:

i. Campaigns: city center efforts and gospel campaign meetings.

ii. Holiday Bible School (VBS): reaching out to children in the area.

iii. Hospital and nursing home visitation.

iv. Summer Camps: reaching out to teens.

v. Bible correspondence courses

vi.   Distribution of literature to doors.

vii. Door Knocking.

viii. Inviting people to church.

ix.   Talking to our own families.

x.   Talking to neighbors.

xi.   Talking to work colleagues.

xii. Serving our community.

Through the years I have been involved in all of the above. They have not all been pleasant experiences, though they have all been entered into with the best of motivations and mustering up every ounce of faith. Not only have I entered into them personally, but through thirty years of working as an evangelist, I have organized such events and encouraged the church as a whole to be busy doing these things. However they have not all been equally successful or beneficial.

Of all of the above, the best are viii through xii.

However, we pour most of our efforts and energies and resources into i-vii. They are, however only a poor substitute for viii-xii. It is viii-xii which are most effective. Christians getting mobilized into action are a thousand times more effective than church programs devised in the preacher's study. A church committed to reaching out is a million times more effective than a distribution program, or an advertising program, or a bill board advertisement. But the church as a whole needs to be equipped to go with the gospel of peace.

Yet it has to be admitted that there is resistance to this, a reticence to step forward and speak.

- There is a fear of rejection.
- There is a fear of my embarrassing myself.
- There is a fear that I am not the kind of representative that Christ should have.

Yet, this is nowhere near as difficult as we imagine it is going to be. Seldom do we experience any real problems as a result of a gentle invitation or inquiry. What is the worst that could possibly happen? The worst is your friend or neighbor saying that they don't think they want to come along right now, or get into a Bible study at this point in their lives. Nothing will be lost. But much could be gained when we think of the priceless gift we have to offer. What can I do?

Have a think now about who you would like to become a Christian and what you could do to encourage them. Begin with praying for them. Think of the ten people you know and love best, who are yet outside of Christ. Then think about what actions you might take beyond prayer.

The next phase will include helping them to understand what the Bible says about becoming a Christian and we will deal with this in future chapters in this book.

Phase three will involve encouraging them to come along to church to see what it is like and benefit from the fellowship, the communion, the teaching, and the whole experience of worship. As Philip said to Nathanael, "Come and see!" (Jn 1:46).

There can be little doubt that evangelism has a lot to do with individual Christians sharing the gospel in a loving way with friends, neighbors and acquaintances. But it is also true that there is a role for the local assembly in all of this. An individual Christian can explain and encourage another to pass through the door, to embrace Christ. But that friend will certainly gaze to the other side of the door and observe those who have already passed through. These are the result of the gospel. Do these products of the gospel seem to have something to sing about, resulting in their lives overflowing with passionate praise? Are they people who are full of the love of the gospel, embracing, welcoming, hospitable, concerned, interested in the lost? Do they engage with me, invite me, accept me? Are they such that I would like to be a part of this family? Lesslie Newbigin states that it is a well established fact, at least in Britain, that the great majority of those who come to faith in Christ come through the witness of a local congregation.[4] In another of his works he referred to the local

---

[4] Op cit. p175

congregation as "the hermeneutic of the gospel". In this rather neat phrase he advances the concept of the crucial and central nature of the local congregation in displaying the force and elegance of the gospel in its outworking in the lives of men and women.

Discussion Points:

1. How, in practice, can the church learn to focus on the Christ in our gospel sharing?

2. Do you think we understand the needs of people in society, and if not what can we do about it?

3. How relevant do you feel the "felt needs" raised in this chapter are?

4. Do you know of others that should be added to that list?

5. How would you see Jesus answering those needs?

6. How would you take the information in the answers to the last five questions and let it impact the way we share the gospel with others?

7. How do we implement the using of methods 8-12 mentioned in this chapter amongst our congregation? Is this a good way to encourage growth in the church or just a way to get the preacher sacked?

8. If we develop a "come and see" approach to evangelism, does this impact the nature of our church meetings?

Chapter Three

What is the Message?

A Message about a Person.

The first thing we must note is that the gospel is not a message about a religion, nor a church system of government, nor a style of worship, nor a plan of study… but essentially it is a message about a Person.

> *26 But an angel of the Lord said to Philip, "Rise and go toward the south to the road that goes down from Jerusalem to Gaza." This is a desert road. 27 And he rose and went. And behold, an Ethiopian, a eunuch, a minister of the Candace, queen of the Ethiopians, in charge of all her treasure, had come to Jerusalem to worship 28 and was returning; seated in his chariot, he was reading the prophet Isaiah. 29 And the Spirit said to Philip, "Go up and join this chariot." 30 So Philip ran to him, and heard him reading Isaiah the prophet, and asked, "Do you understand what you are reading?" 31 And he said, "How can I, unless some one guides me?" And he invited Philip to come up and sit with him. 32 Now the passage of the scripture which he was reading was this: "As a sheep led to the slaughter or a lamb before its shearer is dumb, so he opens not his mouth. 33 In his humiliation justice was denied him. Who can describe*

his generation? For his life is taken up from the earth." [34]
*And the eunuch said to Philip, "About whom, pray, does
the prophet say this, about himself or about some one else?"*
[35] *Then Philip opened his mouth, and beginning with this
scripture he told him the good news of Jesus.* [36] *And as they
went along the road they came to some water, and the
eunuch said, "See, here is water! What is to prevent my being
baptized?"* [38] *And he commanded the chariot to stop, and
they both went down into the water, Philip and the eunuch,
and he baptized him. Acts 8:26-38.*

We note that Philip shared with the eunuch the good news
concerning Jesus. He was a proselyte to the Jewish faith and had just
journeyed hundreds of miles to visit the temple in Jerusalem. They
could have studied the differences between the Jewish and Christian
worship, the differences between the synagogue and the church, the
worship of the temple and the worship of the church, or any number
of other good religious things. However, in effect the beginning point
was none of these things. It was the good news concerning Jesus.
We note in passing that it is the eunuch who brings up baptism. So
the good news concerning Jesus must have included the appropriate
response for man to make.

[18] *For the word of the cross is folly to those who are perishing,
but to us who are being saved it is the power of God.* [19] *For
it is written, "I will destroy the wisdom of the wise, and the
cleverness of the clever I will thwart."* [20] *Where is the wise
man? Where is the scribe? Where is the debater of this age?
Has not God made foolish the wisdom of the world?* [21] *For
since, in the wisdom of God, the world did not know God
through wisdom, it pleased God through the folly of what
we preach to save those who believe.* [22] *For Jews demand
signs and Greeks seek wisdom,* [23] *but **we preach Christ
crucified**, a stumbling block to Jews and folly to Gentiles,* [24]
*but to those who are called, both Jews and Greeks, Christ the
power of God and the wisdom of God.* [25] *For the foolishness*

*of God is wiser than men, and the weakness of God is
stronger than men.   1 Cor 1:18-25.*

*¹ When I came to you, brethren, I did not come proclaiming
to you the testimony of God in lofty words or wisdom. ² For
I decided to know nothing among you **except Jesus Christ
and him crucified.**   1 Cor 2:1-2.*

We note that when Paul went into the city of Corinth, his message
was not philosophy, nor systems, it was a Person. We might say that his
message was not even worldview. He was there to tell the story of Jesus.
It was the same thing when Peter preached the gospel in Jerusalem
seven weeks after the crucifixion.

*²⁹ "Brethren, I may say to you confidently of the patriarch
David that he both died and was buried, and his tomb is
with us to this day. ³⁰ Being therefore a prophet, and knowing
that God had sworn with an oath to him that he would set
one of his descendants upon his throne, ³¹ he foresaw and spoke
of the resurrection of the Christ, that he was not abandoned
to Hades, nor did his flesh see corruption. ³² This Jesus God
raised up, and of that we all are witnesses. ³³ Being therefore
exalted at the right hand of God, and having received from
the Father the promise of the Holy Spirit, he has poured out
this which you see and hear. ³⁴ For David did not ascend into
the heavens; but he himself says, 'The Lord said to my Lord,
Sit at my right hand, ³⁵ till I make thy enemies a stool for thy
feet.' ³⁶ Let all the house of Israel therefore know assuredly that
God has made him both Lord and Christ, this Jesus whom you
crucified." Acts 2:29-36.*

Here in the first gospel sermon ever preached, we see how Peter
stands up before his fellow Jews and focuses their attention on
the Christ. Jesus is the core of his message. Christ was crucified in
accordance with the prophetic message. Messiah has come. And the
crucified Christ was the heart of it.

And Jesus also made this His theme. He refers to His crucifixion many times. There were a number of times when He refers to it, calling it being "lifted up". By this He means lifted up on the Cross. Jesus saw this as the heart of why He had come and the heart of what the disciples would share concerning Him.

> *14 And as Moses lifted up the serpent in the wilderness, so must the Son of man be lifted up, 15 that whoever believes in him may have eternal life." Jn 3:14-15.*

> *28 So Jesus said, "When you have lifted up the Son of man, then you will know that I am he, and that I do nothing on my own authority but speak thus as the Father taught me. 29 And he who sent me is with me; he has not left me alone, for I always do what is pleasing to him." 30 As he spoke thus, many believed in him. Jn 8:28-30.*

> *31 Now is the judgment of this world, now shall the ruler of this world be cast out; 32 and I, when I am lifted up from the earth, will draw all men to myself." 33 He said this to show by what death he was to die. 34 The crowd answered him, "We have heard from the law that the Christ remains for ever. How can you say that the Son of man must be lifted up? Who is this Son of man?" 35 Jesus said to them, "The light is with you for a little longer. Walk while you have the light, lest the darkness overtake you; he who walks in the darkness does not know where he goes. 36 While you have the light, believe in the light, that you may become sons of light." Jn 12:31-36.*

Jesus predicts that it is the cross which will draw men to Him. And when you think about why you became a Christian... what has made the difference in your life then you have to conclude that it is the Cross that makes the difference.

It really is all about the death of Jesus and how that death makes life possible for me. He has died that I might live. Indeed this thought is innate in Old and New Testaments alike. The Passover lamb sealed the redemption of Israel. It was the blood of the Passover lamb painted on the doorposts that made the deliverance of Israel possible. It was when God saw the blood that He passed over the houses where Israel was to be found, and in that blood they found their redemption.

> *The blood shall be a sign for you, upon the houses where you are; and when I see the blood, I will pass over you, and no plague shall fall upon you to destroy you, when I smite the land of Egypt. Ex 12:13.*

And Jesus has become our Passover Lamb.

> *[29] The next day he saw Jesus coming toward him, and said, "Behold, the Lamb of God, who takes away the sin of the world! Jn 1:29*

> *For Christ, our paschal lamb, has been sacrificed. 1 Cor 5:7.*

Jesus as our Passover Lamb, declares the relevance of His sacrificial death for us. It is only in His death we find our redemptive story realized.

The story of the Day of Atonement points to the sacrifice of Jesus being the central act of history. On that day the high priest would lay hands on the head of a goat as he confessed the sins of the nation over the goat. The guilt of the nation was imputed to the goat and then it was driven from the camp. It was sent off into the wilderness never to return to the camp again and symbolically bore the sins of the nation far from their door. That guilt would never return to them because of the graciousness of God in imputing the sins to what the King James Version called the "scapegoat". The scapegoat bore the sins of the nation.

> *[20] "And when he has made an end of atoning for the holy place and the tent of meeting and the altar, he shall present the live goat; [21] and Aaron shall lay both his hands upon the head of the live goat, and confess over him all the iniquities of the people of Israel, and all their transgressions, all their*

*sins; and he shall put them upon the head of the goat, and
send him away into the wilderness by the hand of a man
who is in readiness. ²² The goat shall bear all their iniquities
upon him to a solitary land; and he shall let the goat go in
the wilderness. Lev 16:20-22.*

Jesus has become our scapegoat. We find our salvation in His
action of bearing our sins and taking them far from us by His grace.
He who knew no sin, became sin for us, in order that we might
become the righteousness of God. (2 Cor 5:21)

Hence when we set out to share the gospel with the world, what
we have to grasp is that the message we are sharing is about the Christ,
and it is about Him crucified. Who could have predicted that so
many people would want to go and watch a movie in two ancient
foreign languages with sub titles and that people would flock in their
thousands and thousands to watch it? And yet the Passion pulled in
such audiences because the message of the Cross is compelling.

The Source of our Message:

What is the source of our message? How do we share the good
news of Jesus and Him Crucified with the world? Are we to write
provocative stories about it? Listen to this incident in the ministry of
Jesus.

*⁴ And when a great crowd came together and people from
town after town came to him, he said in a parable: ⁵ "A
sower went out to sow his seed; and as he sowed, some fell
along the path, and was trodden under foot, and the birds
of the air devoured it. ⁶ And some fell on the rock; and as
it grew up, it withered away, because it had no moisture.
⁷ And some fell among thorns; and the thorns grew with
it and choked it. ⁸ And some fell into good soil and grew,
and yielded a hundredfold." As he said this, he called out,
"He who has ears to hear, let him hear." ⁹ And when his
disciples asked him what this parable meant, ¹⁰ he said, "To
you it has been given to know the secrets of the kingdom of*

God; but for others they are in parables, so that seeing they may not see, and hearing they may not understand. [11] Now the parable is this: The seed is the word of God. [12] The ones along the path are those who have heard; then the devil comes and takes away the word from their hearts, that they may not believe and be saved. [13] And the ones on the rock are those who, when they hear the word, receive it with joy; but these have no root, they believe for a while and in time of temptation fall away. [14] And as for what fell among the thorns, they are those who hear, but as they go on their way they are choked by the cares and riches and pleasures of life, and their fruit does not mature. [15] And as for that in the good soil, they are those who, hearing the word, hold it fast in an honest and good heart, and bring forth fruit with patience. Lke 8:4-15.

We note that what is to be planted is the seed and the seed is the Word of God.

[22] Having purified your souls by your obedience to the truth for a sincere love of the brethren, love one another earnestly from the heart. [23] You have been born anew, not of perishable seed but of imperishable, through the living and abiding word of God; [24] for "All flesh is like grass and all its glory like the flower of grass. The grass withers, and the flower falls, [25] but the word of the Lord abides for ever." That word is the good news which was preached to you. [1] So put away all malice and all guile and insincerity and envy and all slander. [2] Like newborn babes, long for the pure spiritual milk, that by it you may grow up to salvation; [3] for you have tasted the kindness of the Lord. 1 Pet 1:22 – 2:3

Note what this passage says about the Word of God…

- We are born again through the Word of God.
- It is not just an ordinary book, but a living Word.

- It will never go out of date or become powerless because it is an eternal Word.

- That Word was what was preached to those first Christians and brought them into Christ.

- The Word was the good news preached.

- It is that same Word which enables us to grow spiritually, it provides the milk that sustains us as Christians.

> ³⁰ *Now Jesus did many other signs in the presence of the disciples, which are not written in this book;* ³¹ *but these are written that you may believe that Jesus is the Christ, the Son of God, and that believing you may have life in his name. Jn 20:30-31.*

We shall be returning to these verses later in this work but we note that the purpose that John wrote his gospel account was in order to produce faith.

That is, as we present Jesus through the gospel account, we are preaching the Word of God, we are presenting the crucified Christ, and in seeing this Crucified Christ, people are brought to faith in Him, and through faith in Him, life in Him.

Discussion:

Embodied in this chapter are some thoughts that affect what we do in gospel sharing. There are fundamental principles in gospel sharing that we must learn before we can be successful. What does all of the above suggest to us about how we should share the gospel?

1. That gospel sharing must be grounded in the Word of God. It is that Word which brings life.

2. That gospel sharing must be grounded in the gospel accounts which share the message of Christ with us and lead to faith.

3. That we must have a focus in our evangelism and the focus must be Christ.

4. Like many in New Testament times, people in general do not know Christ or really that much about Him; hence our evangelistic efforts must be centered on sharing the person of Christ.

5. Hence the central thrust of our gospel outreach must be centered on the Bible and centered on the Christ of the Bible... how do we implement a strategy based on that?

You may also want to add your own observations at this stage.

6.

7.

Chapter Four
Engaging with the Text

Introduction: The Two Key Ingredients

All twelve of the efforts described previously, which describe our attempts at sharing the gospel are geared towards the establishing of a home Bible study. In my experience a home Bible study is a crucial part of the process. Only with some kind of systematic teaching in a setting that permits questions to be asked and dialogue to take place can we expect to lead people to the most momentous decision of their lives.

There are two factors which must be present for the optimum experience to result. A home study must be taking place that allows us to present the Christ, and the searcher should be attending worship services to meet the family we hope they are going to be added to.

I have known situations where the individual is involved in a home Bible study and decides to become a Christian. We have taken the person to the church building to baptize them into Christ and been utterly amazed when this was the one and only time an appearance was made in the church building. The reasons for this may be complex and we may not understand all of them but it is clear that if someone does not see the need to participate in communal worship before their baptism, often they will not see the need for it after baptism either. And simply because we understand the connection, we can join up all the dots because we have a sense of the big picture, does not mean to say that everybody can. Many in society today have no concept of the big picture and they do not and perhaps cannot join up the dots.

The other side of the coin is also common. That is, we have many people who come along to worship services. They are not Christians. But perhaps they are married to a Christian or are the son or daughter of a Christian. They attend services but there is no personal Bible study in progress. I have seen this situation go on for years without any noticeable progress towards that person becoming a Christian.

The two things work together. A home Bible study is essential for the sharing of the gospel. There is something magical about the home Bible study in which the right kind of dialogue is possible for the effective sharing of faith. Monologue is not anything like as effective, though perhaps you might think that a strange statement for a gospel preacher to make. I think preaching is important. It is important in leading someone into a home Bible study in which they may make a decision for Christ. Sometimes it is important for those who have already taken part in a home Bible study to find the urgency from preaching to take that decision. The home Bible study makes that decision an informed decision. Further, there may be the feeling in the minds of some seekers that their home is more like neutral ground for them. It might not seem right to challenge the message in the midst of the church building. It is almost an act of sacrilege to do so. I have these real questions in my mind but I couldn't raise these questions in the shadow of the pulpit or the altar or the sacred shades cast by the stained glass windows. But in my own home, I can raise the real issues that are on my heart and in my mind.

Also, in a home Bible study there is the opportunity to share the message of the gospel over several sessions to allow time for the seeker to absorb the great and enormous issues of the gospel. In the New Testament there are instances of people becoming Christians, responding to the gospel preaching and being baptized on the basis, it appears, of one sermon. Yet when we examine the circumstances we find that it is not as simple as that. In certain circumstances the whole process was assisted by an apostolic miracle, or the hearers were Jews who were specially prepared by the prophetic ministries of the Old Testament and the dynamic preaching of John the Baptist. These people had their minds tuned in to a gospel worldview.

But for most people today, they need the opportunity to ask lots of questions and chew over the gospel message. Dialogue and discussion will be invaluable to making sense of a new worldview. They need time to meet this Jesus and drink in the new wine of this wonderful message of the Messiah King who has come.

There is also something magical about worship. It can be a very powerful thing for those who are not yet Christians to enter into a worship service where real worship is taking place.

- When Christians pour out their hearts in ardent praise,

- and sincere prayers are offered up from hearts which are in fellowship with God,

- and emblems are taken in memory of a Savior's love

- and the Word of God is preached in all its power, purity and simplicity...

- then those outside of Christ are aware that something significant is happening.

They are impressed by the sincerity and "realness" of it all. And the whole purpose of worship is to magnify the Lord and under such magnification the seeker after God sees more clearly the greatness of God.

One very widely held view is that spirituality is good. Even in this materialistic society, the idea of being spiritual has very wide acceptance, much more so than being religious. And so for a visitor to observe spiritual worship, this is very powerful testimony to the validity of Christianity. But there is by no means a consensus on the definition of the word spirituality. To some it means anything which leads to an emotional experience, or gives satisfaction to the emotional nature of man. To others it is that which leads to the person-centered meditations of quiet times (whether or not this involves what we might think of as prayer). To some it is the ecstasy of an exuberant worship experience. And perhaps the only common ground is that for most people spirituality is something which is felt.

However, does worship have to be exuberant or an ecstatic performance for it to be considered spiritual? Perhaps these things stem from a confusion over the spiritual gifts which were temporary gifts to the few, and spiritual fruit which was a permanent evidence of the presence of the Spirit of God in the Christian and in the church. A careful reading of Galatians chapter five gives us a snapshot of the nature of the fruit of the Spirit and hence by definition that which is spiritual. According to Peter (1 Pet 1:22ff), the action of the Word of God in the hearts of men and women is to be likened to seed planted in the heart which brings forth life and growth. We are born again of the living and abiding Word of God. This leads to fruit being borne, fruit which comes from the Spirit of God indwelling the Christian. The Spirit of God is alive and well and active in the church. And hence it should not surprise us that when visitors come into our worship, in the midst of the sincere and heart-felt worship of those who are temples of the Holy Spirit, it is noticeable that they are in the midst of spiritual worship. This testimony to the realness of our new life in Christ is very powerful.

The Home Study:

The key to the home study is the text. Though some people are more dynamic than others and it is good if we can use our whole personality in the service of the Master, the home study is not about you. Indeed it must not be about you.

This is why none of us should be afraid to serve in this area. It does not depend upon me, my knowledge, my magnetism. It is about the magnetism of the Master. Jesus said that He would draw all men to Himself by the cross.

I have known of those whose performance in home Bible studies was all about themselves. And unfortunately when the process was over they may or may not gather disciples for themselves. These are disciples not of Jesus but of the teacher. And when the teacher messes up, or lets them down as inevitably he must, then the people are gone. I have known those who have bullied others into accepting the gospel, but that does not last either. For at some stage another imperative will come along that bullies them out of their discipleship. It must be a free will decision. It must be an informed decision based on believing the gospel.

> *[14] But how are men to call upon him in whom they have not believed? And how are they to believe in him of whom they have never heard? And how are they to hear without a preacher? [15] And how can men preach unless they are sent? As it is written, "How beautiful are the feet of those who preach good news!" [16] But they have not all obeyed the gospel; for Isaiah says, "Lord, who has believed what he has heard from us?" [17] So faith comes from what is heard, and what is heard comes by the preaching of Christ. Rom 10:14-17.*

Remembering the words of the Apostle John in 20:30-31, we realize that the purpose of the gospel record is to lead others to faith in Christ. Many times in my own Christian life, when I have felt low in faith, I have turned again to the gospels (particularly that of John) and found my faith rebuilt again as I read the ancient words of life. I am reintroduced to Jesus and I remember again why my heart thrilled to see Him and to know Him. This is no dead book. It is the living and active Word of God that brings us from death to life through the gospel.

Peter says that we are born anew by the Word of God planted in our hearts. It is a life giving Word.

Hence we see the importance of what we are calling engaging with the text. There has to be a life giving connection between us and the Word. But what do we mean by engaging? Let us make some observations…

1. It has something to do with reading the text. This is to state the obvious. And we are now living in a society where reading is in decline. People don't read books like they used to. Public libraries are increasingly more involved in the process of lending out CDs, computer games and other electronic resources rather than books. But we need to encourage people to read the text. In my home studies we read the text together. If the person is not educationally disadvantaged in any way I get them to share in the reading of the text aloud. I also encourage them to be reading through the gospel record on their

own in between studies. The more I can encourage them to read the text the easier my task becomes in leading them to Christ. Indeed they are being led by the Holy Spirit to Christ in their reading for this Word is inspired of the Holy Spirit.

2. But it is something more than just reading. It is possible to scan a newspaper, or novel without truly engaging with the text of it. Cursory reading is not enough. We need the individual to become personally involved in the text they are reading. We might describe it as **considered reading of the text.**

3. However, in effect this engagement goes much further than that. This is where the use of dialogue is necessary to get the seeker to really consider the message of the text. I ask them questions…

- If you had been one of the disciples in the boat in the midst of this storm, how do you think you would have felt?

- What do you think you would have said to the sleeping figure of Jesus in the corner of the boat?

- How would you have described this stilling of the storm to others back home when you returned?

- How do you think you would tell this experience to your grandchildren?

- What does this incident teach us about Jesus?

- How do you think this experience made the disciples feel about Jesus?

By these means we are encouraging the seeker to start to put themselves into the story. The more they can do this, the more this story becomes their story.

4. Engaging the text is about letting the story of Jesus penetrate into our minds and consciousness till it fuses with

our own story. We infuse the study with prayer, and we encourage the consideration of the text, as the living Word of God that reveals the eternal Logos of God to us. By placing ourselves on the scene and in the story we allow that story to speak to us as never before. Who is this Jesus? What did He do? What does that say about Him? How did Jesus deal with people? What does that say about how He wants to deal with us? In a miraculous way, the story of the gospel doesn't just inform us of historical facts. It does more, much more. It invites our involvement in the story, draws us into the story. Who can truly engage with the story of the crucifixion of the Lord and His resurrection and not be incorporated in the story? We feel the impact of the nails and the horror of the scourging. We bristle with indignation at the mocking of the soldiers and the crown of thorns, the mock royal robe, and the heartless gambling over his meager possessions. Reading the Bible is not just about information gathering. On one level, it is about information but so much more. We feel the emotions of God the Father, caring about me so much that He was willing to watch His one-of-a-kind Son suffering in such a powerful way in order to accomplish my redemption. We see and feel the outpouring of sacrificial love that came from the Savior, as questions were asked of Him. Are you prepared to go this far for redemption's sake? Yes? Well what about even this far? Yes? Then what are you prepared to give for the story of redemption? What is that Jesus? You are prepared to give it all, give everything, give your very life? And thus His story becomes our story. The gospel story does not just tell a story, it invites our absorption into this story… indeed it invites this story to absorb us into its fabric. Faith comes by hearing. And the presentation of the Christ from the Scriptures is powerful.

This matter of engagement is at the heart of finding faith through the text of Scripture. There are times when we are so concerned about the translation of the language and wishing it to be as accurate a translation as possible that we lose sight of the message of the passage. It is interesting to look at *The Message*, a modern translation by Eugene Peterson. Here we see a modern version of the Scriptures which is quite unlike others. It is obvious on reading it that it is no literal translation. But it is also obvious that Peterson gets to the real nitty-gritty of the passage for us today. If the verse has not been translated word for word, it must be said that so often the concepts have been, thought for thought. Peterson makes it clear that the process has involved becoming immersed in the text and attempting to paraphrase the text in our own words for today. The goal is to communicate the thought of the passage in our vocabulary and language.

In his excellent little work *Eat This Book*, Peterson recounts how this translation came into being. He speaks of countless group bible classes where the order of the day was for every member to come up with a "translation" that speaks to them from the heart of the message. Can it be that what the man in the street needs more than anything else is for the Bible to speak to him in the language of the common man?

Before we can truly engage with the text we have to understand it. We have to see it in our own language and vocabulary, we have to eat and drink it, wake and sleep it, drink its depths and let it breathe into our nostrils the breath of life. And before we can teach it to others we need to understand the text as well as we are able. We have to look up unfamiliar terms or customs until we understand the bones of the passage. This will allow us to write out what the passage is about and what it is saying to us in our own language.

Then we need to invite the person we are studying with to so engage with the text that they can express the passage in their own words. And in doing so our primary toolbox is made up entirely of questions. Open-ended questions that invite participation and involvement help this seeker to really engage with the text. How do you see this passage? What feelings does Jesus' statement provoke in you? What do you like about the characters in this story? What don't you like?

When the Word of God is allowed to speak to us in this way it becomes very powerful. The word of the gospel truly is the power of God unto salvation. In fact I am saying that this is so powerful that it replaces much of the need for a defense of the Scriptures in other fields. If it does not *completely* replace it then it does to all intents and purposes. And often a cursory discussion in the field of evidences of inspiration, or creation, or even the existence of God at a later date in the study is all that is required. This may sound philosophically wrong. But you need to take into account the faith building properties of allowing the Word of God to speak to us.

But we might object, there are so many problems with a Darwinian worldview, obstructing understanding, corrupting the frame of reference, and obscuring the message of the gospel. Of course, all of that is true. However the solution is not so much a program of education as it is an introduction. When someone is truly introduced to Jesus then it changes their frame of reference. It adjusts their worldview. Although there may be much learning still required, nevertheless it is the introduction which is key to the solution.

This story is in effect a great saga, encompassing a number of stories and every one of them is vital to who we are. There is the Creation Story, the Fall Story, the Redemption Story and the Regeneration Story. And these are stories recounted in the Bible but they are stories that define our identity. It is our own story. But if such a transformation is to take place, it must take place and can only take place on the basis of a meeting with Jesus.

When conducting a home Bible study with the aim of sharing the gospel message, I would be prepared to discuss the existence of God, the inspiration of the Scriptures, Creation and other issues when raised by the individual, because these are good questions which impinge upon the story, and impinge upon the worldview. But if a brief discussion of them can suffice, putting it off until later often means that there is a much more sympathetic ear to listen to the arguments once something of the loveliness of the Lord, the majesty of the Master has been perceived by engaging with the text. For when we have tasted of the goodness of God and the loving kindness of the Lord Christ, it seems that some matters which once disturbed us do not seem quite so disturbing any longer. Often when looked at through eyes of faith the problems seem to melt as snowmen under a blazing sun. Paul talks about this in terms of the renewal of our mind.

² Do not be conformed to this world but be transformed by the renewal of your mind, that you may prove what is the will of God, what is good and acceptable and perfect. Rom 12:2.

Our primary purpose is to share the story of Jesus. All else must take its place in turn. For once the story has been told, and adopted by the seeker, then these other matters take on a new lesser importance, because we look from an entirely new perspective. We soar upwards, embracing the Messiah and from this spiritual height we see everything in a new perspective.

In the chapters which follow I will illustrate this methodology by means of looking at a series of actual lessons I use in the home Bible study. Remember that the purpose is to introduce someone to Jesus. The more they see Him, the more they can begin to see the story of their own redemption, and the more their worldview is changed. And the big picture that emerges is the one in which we see God as our Creator, Redeemer and Friend. And in this worldview we have a coherent picture of who we are, where we are, where we are going, and how we are going to get there. But none of that is possible until we have seen Jesus.

In writing this book, my purpose is not to present a philosophical treatise. It is not to push the boundaries of understanding of these philosophical issues. But this is a book written by a simple herald of the good news, sharing a view of gospel preaching in this post Christian world. And so there may be matters which are brought up which the highly knowledgeable may think is "nothing new". Yet I am writing the book I wish someone had handed me thirty years ago when I began on the marvelous adventure of the work of evangelism, and attempting to share the unsearchable riches of Christ with a world that knows not Christ.

Discussion Points:

1. What do you think a visitor would derive from a visit to our worship services?

2. Do we come to worship to give or to receive?

3. Why is it good to encourage those we are studying with to attend worship services?

4. Why is Bible reading and engaging with the text emphasized as the all- important factor?

5. Can you think of some questions you could use that would help people to truly engage with the text?

6. Is encouraging the person we are studying with to read the Bible on his own as well as in the study a good idea?

7. Is Christian evidences something that is good to study?

8. Who can be an effective evangelist of the good things of God?

9. How should we prepare ourselves to be a herald of the gospel?

10. In a previous generation, churches thought about their responsibility to evangelize and organized gospel meetings for that purpose. Discuss that as a strategy for today.

Part Two

The Home Bible Study

Chapter Five

The First Sign: Turning Water into Wine

THE NEXT EIGHT CHAPTERS ARE in effect the model for a series of eight presentations that can be made in the homes of seekers after truth. They are a structured approach to sharing the gospel, sharing the Person of Christ with others. And as such, by an examination of these seven signs, and the ultimate or eighth sign, we are introducing a precious soul to Jesus. Each lesson can be modeled by the evangelist to suit the individual needs of the person who seeks. Salvation in Christ, to each individual whoever they are, and whatever state they find themselves, is the answer. Each sign must be considered in turn, for each study builds faith in the One who came from heaven to redeem us. To many of you who read this work, these lessons may seem to be "old hat". Having been a member of the church for some years, these stories and events are as familiar to us as a favorite golfing hat, and as comfortable as your armchair. But we forget that to the man out there in the Post-Christian world, these stories are new and exciting. They have never heard them, never read them, and never considered them. The notes contained in each chapter are there to aid your background knowledge. Since the method of delivery is dialogue and not monologue, they are not related here in order that you might read them out to another pilgrim on the pathway of faith but to stimulate us to think and prepare ourselves before the home study to tell the story, and share something of the majesty of the Master.

In the home Bible study we need to engage with the text. Our chief message concerns the person of Jesus. This suggests very simply that our main texts for Bible study will come from somewhere in the four gospel accounts. Some express preference for one account or another, or perhaps some combination of the four. However I find it easier when studying with someone if all of our readings, or most of them come from the same book. Those who are ignorant of the Scriptures always find it difficult to locate Bible references. They just don't know how to begin to find a passage. Is it Old Testament or New?

My preferred methodology is to stick to one book. And my preference is the gospel of John. If this is the case then all a person has to do is to locate the appropriate chapter and all the chapters are in order and easy to find. Of course if questions come up I am prepared to go to wherever that question is answered in the Bible to show that there is a clear Biblical answer to the question, but as for the main thrust of the study, I will concentrate on this one gospel account.

With that in mind, let us turn to a series of lessons on the gospel of John and see what we can learn from looking at these passages with fresh eyes.

John stands out as the gospel (more than any other), which presents Jesus as Son of God. Indeed John points out that this is his whole purpose in writing. There are many themes running through the gospel of John and each is worthy of our consideration. These are just some of the themes:

- The Eternal Word (Logos) of God (God became flesh)
- Light
- Life
- Love
- Truth

We know that Jesus performed many miracles during his earthly ministry, too many to mention, too many to count.

> *[24] This is the disciple who is bearing witness to these things, and who has written these things; and we know that his*

testimony is true. ²⁵ *But there are also many other things which Jesus did; were every one of them to be written, I suppose that the world itself could not contain the books that would be written. John 21:24-25.*

Just how many miracles did Jesus perform? It is too difficult to estimate, too difficult to count. Consider the following passages.

²⁴ So his fame spread throughout all Syria, and they brought him all the sick, those afflicted with various diseases and pains, demoniacs, epileptics, and paralytics, and he healed them. Matt 4:24.

¹⁶ That evening they brought to him many who were possessed with demons; and he cast out the spirits with a word, and healed all who were sick. Matt 8:16.

¹⁵ Jesus, aware of this, withdrew from there. And many followed him, and he healed them all, Matt 12:15.

¹⁴ As he went ashore he saw a great throng; and he had compassion on them, and healed their sick. Matt 14:14.

³⁰ And great crowds came to him, bringing with them the lame, the maimed, the blind, the dumb, and many others, and they put them at his feet, and he healed them, Matt 15:30.

¹ Now when Jesus had finished these sayings, he went away from Galilee and entered the region of Judea beyond the Jordan; ² and large crowds followed him, and he healed them there. Matt 19:1-2.

¹⁴ And the blind and the lame came to him in the temple, and he healed them. Matt 21:14

These are excerpts only from the gospel of Matthew and we note that there were a number of occasions when many sick people were brought to Jesus and He healed every one of them. Would it be too much of a stretch of the imagination that on some of these occasions there were perhaps twenty people, or fifty or even a hundred people? After all, everyone with a sick relative would want to avail themselves of this marvelous opportunity. So it would seem that the number of the miracles of Jesus would easily run into hundreds and even, some might argue thousands when every miracle is included.

But of the multitudes of miracles and signs that Jesus performed, very surprisingly, only seven are recorded by John.[5] This is utterly amazing. How can it be that this gospel record tells us only of seven signs?

> [30] *Now Jesus did many other signs in the presence of the disciples, which are not written in this book;* [31] *but these are written that you may believe that Jesus is the Christ, the Son of God, and that believing you may have life in his name.*
> *Jn 20:30-31.*

The Holy Spirit speaking through John considers that these seven are enough! If we are aware of these seven then these alone should convince us that Jesus is the Christ, the Son of God. These alone should lead us to faith.

In the next few chapters, I thought it might be profitable to look at these seven signs and think about them, consider these since God wanted us to consider them. And God's idea was that in considering them we might be brought to faith, established in our faith, strengthened in our faith in Him. Let us look at the first sign:

---

[5] There are some who would maintain that there are eight signs. However the number seven comes from a way of analysing John's gospel in a different way. The gospel may be thought of as presenting the deity of the Lord Jesus Christ in seven great signs. This is followed by the ultimate sign (the sign of Jonah). The crucifixion and resurrection of Jesus is the ultimate sign. Following the resurrection there are resurrection appearances which confirm the faith of the apostles in the risen Christ. The "eighth" sign (John21) is really in the context of a resurrection proof or appearance.

The First Sign

> *[1] On the third day there was a marriage at Cana in Galilee,*
> *and the mother of Jesus was there; [2] Jesus also was invited*
> *to the marriage, with his disciples. [3] When the wine failed,*
> *the mother of Jesus said to him, "They have no wine." [4] And*
> *Jesus said to her, "O woman, what have you to do with me?*
> *My hour has not yet come." [5] His mother said to the servants,*
> *"Do whatever he tells you." [6] Now six stone jars were standing*
> *there, for the Jewish rites of purification, each holding twenty*
> *or thirty gallons. [7] Jesus said to them, "Fill the jars with*
> *water." And they filled them up to the brim. [8] He said to*
> *them, "Now draw some out, and take it to the steward of the*
> *feast." So they took it. [9] When the steward of the feast tasted*
> *the water now become wine, and did not know where it came*
> *from (though the servants who had drawn the water knew),*
> *the steward of the feast called the bridegroom [10] and said to*
> *him, "Every man serves the good wine first; and when men*
> *have drunk freely, then the poor wine; but you have kept the*
> *good wine until now." [11] This, the first of his signs, Jesus did*
> *at Cana in Galilee, and manifested his glory; and his disciples*
> *believed in him.   Jn 2:1-11.*

As we look at this reading, we want to become as familiar as possible with this passage before sharing it with others. What happens? Who are the principal players in this scene? Are there things I don't understand? What kind of questions would this story raise in the minds of others who are not Bible readers? We have to wrestle with the story first ourselves. Sharing the gospel is all about sharing the message of the text and we need to take time to become familiar with the text. Let us take a few moments to consider this.

1.   The guests!

The scene is a village quite near to Nazareth the place of Jesus' childhood. The occasion is a marriage feast. And as we read the passage clearly we see something quite interesting.

the mother of Jesus was there; [2] *Jesus also was invited to the marriage, with his disciples*

We note that it does not say that Mary was invited. It says that she was there. Jesus and His disciples were invited but Mary was there. It becomes clear that she has some official function to perform at the feast. Some later writings suggest that the wedding involved relatives of Mary. It is clear that she has something to do with serving at the feast for she is aware of the background dilemma and the embarrassing situation that had developed.

2. The supplies

It was not the case that the people of the feast had become drunk. In fact drunkenness was a great disgrace and they commonly drank their wine in a mixture composing two parts wine to three parts water. But the failure of supplies would have been regarded as a great disgrace because hospitality in the East is a sacred duty, even today. And for the provision at a wedding to run out would be a terrible shame and disgrace for the bride and bridegroom. Indeed it would not be too great an exaggeration to say that it would be a humiliation for this to occur.

3. No Joseph.

It is also interesting to note that there is no mention of Joseph anywhere in the story. Would he not have been at the wedding? It was near to Nazareth and Mary was there, and Jesus was there. But there is no mention of Joseph. Indeed there is no mention of Joseph anywhere in the Scriptures after the trip with Jesus to the temple when Jesus was around twelve years of age. Most scholars and commentators have concluded that Joseph had died. Indeed this might explain why Jesus, as the eldest of the children in this family had stayed home until the age of thirty to care for his mother and younger sisters and brothers until he could leave the care of the home in his brothers' charge whilst He left to fulfill His ministry from the Heavenly Father, and His eternal destiny. The New Testament makes it clear that there were four brothers of the Lord who are named and a plural number of sisters.

4. The Water

It was because of Jewish custom and practice that a great deal of water was required for such a gathering. First of all, every guest would require their feet washed before joining in the festivities. Roads were hot and dusty and footwear consisted of open sandals. And so it was the custom to offer foot washing to all visitors. In our culture it would be custom to offer a cup of tea because in our climate visitors will arrive cold and wet most of the time, so a hot cup of tea is regarded as a common courtesy. In the Biblical culture it would be to offer feet washing. Hence at a large gathering such as this wedding, much water would be required to wash the feet of the guests.

Further Jewish custom demanded that there would be a ceremonial washing of the hands before eating. This had nothing to do with physical cleanliness or hygiene. It was a religious act. The hands were first of all held pointing up the way and water was poured on from the top and it had to run down to the wrists or off at the elbow. Then the hands were held pointing down the way and the water was poured on from the wrist or elbow and allowed to run down and off the fingers. Then finally each palm was cleansed by rubbing it with the fist of the other hand. Jewish ceremonial law required that this should be done, and for some, not only at the beginning of the meal but also between courses. And for the water itself to be considered ceremonially clean it had to be stored in these stone jars. It was for this foot washing and hand cleansing that such a large supply of water was necessary.

Indeed, according to the wording used in the passage, there would have been between 120 and 180 gallons of water capacity in these jars.

5. The Steward.

Finally we note the steward of the feast. His role would have been generally to manage the feast. The serving and supplying would have been his ultimate responsibility. Indeed we might think of him today as like a kind of head-waiter or Maitre D of the feast.

We note his reaction to the water made into wine, not knowing where it had come from. This was much finer wine than had been supplied earlier. And he comments…

"Every man serves the good wine first; and when men have drunk freely, then the poor wine; but you have kept the good wine until now."

It would be a mistake to think that he means that the custom was to get everyone drunk then they would not know what they were drinking. He is simply referring to the ability of the palate to distinguish the quality of fine wine after some time of drinking inferior quality of wine.

He is amazed; for the quality of this newly arrived wine is much better than what had gone before. Why not serve the best wine first.

Jesus and His Mother

It is also interesting to notice is the interface between Jesus and His mother in this incident.

1. Mary's Faith.

One of the bright shining lights of this incident is the faith of Mary. The wine had run out. And there are many wedding guests. Where did Mary think Jesus would get enough wine to solve this problem? What led her to believe that Jesus could solve it?

We commented earlier that Joseph, we think, has died and for the past many years Jesus has been the man of the house. And so perhaps it was natural for Mary to turn to Jesus with this difficult problem. Who else would she go to? Perhaps she should have gone to the steward in charge of the feast. Perhaps she should have spoken to the principal family concerned. But instead she turns to Jesus as she would do in the event of some calamity at home.

But why did she imagine he could help in this circumstance? Did she think that Jesus would perform some miracle? This was his first miracle so that would not have been based on having seen Jesus perform miracles previously. Yet she had faith in Jesus to be able to solve the problem. This is clear from what she subsequently says to those who served…

5 His mother said to the servants, "Do whatever he tells you."

Mary expected that Jesus would do something! Perhaps this was based on…

- events surrounding His birth.
- His perfect character- God in the flesh.

But the faith of Mary in the ability of Jesus to solve the problem is one of the highlights of this passage.

2. Jesus' speech.

It would be good for us in passing to comment on how Jesus speaks to His mother for in our translation it comes over unnecessarily harsh and gives quite the wrong impression.

> *"O woman, what have you to do with me? My hour has not yet come."*

The words are a translation of the original but there are three points which are worthy of making with reference to this:

a) There is no indication of the tone in which they were uttered. We could say this first phrase in a hundred different tones and the import would be totally different in each case.

b) The word woman seems awfully cold and somewhat of a put down in our English translation but the original did not carry any of that. Remember how he used the same address when he hung on the cross and in fact it was a term which carried with it the idea of respect. Barclay says that we have no equivalent term in English to this usage in the Greek. He suggests that the word, "Lady" perhaps suggests the idea of respect better.

c) The phrase "what have you to do with me" loses a great deal in the translation. It was not the cold disrespectful statement that it appears to be in our English version. It was capable of being understood in different ways depending on the tone used. If it were uttered sharply and in anger then it would be understood the way we might imagine from first reading. But it was also capable of being understood in the sense, "don't worry you don't understand what is going on, leave it to me." Perhaps we might utter the words, "What are we going to do with you", in a similar way.

It is clear that Mary does not understand how Jesus will solve the problem. And though He submitted Himself to Mary and Joseph in His childhood, the decision as to when and how He will enter into His miraculous ministry is not hers to determine. She has made the need known. He will decide how and where He will use His powers as Son of God.

Jesus and the Sign.

It is time for us to consider the spiritual implications of this remarkable miracle. Let us look at some lessons we must not miss from this passage.

1. The Quality of the Grace of God

Note what we learn about the quality of the grace of God. When there was an embarrassing lack of wine, God supplied not just any old wine but the finest of wines. It was an astounding quality of wine which should have been served first when the palate was at its most discriminating.

This tells us that when God takes a hand, we can expect the finest of results. When we have some trouble or calamity in our own lives what we can expect is not just any old partial solution where God provides us a patch up, where God supplies a piece of cardboard to patch up the broken window of our lives. No what He will supply will be the finest window that we can imagine. It is triple glazed, it is draught free, it is of the finest materials. This is what God can and does supply into our lives.

In fact whenever God comes into the life of an individual, there is a change which we might liken to turning water into wine. Wherever Jesus goes, wherever Jesus is welcomed in, it is like turning water into wine. If you will become a disciple, a disciple of the Lord Jesus Christ, then the water of your life will be turned into the wine of the spiritually blessed life for this is the quality of the grace of God.

2.   The superabundant quantity of the grace of God.

Further we notice that Jesus provided a wonderful abundance of wine. One wonders whether 180 gallons of wine were really necessary for this wedding feast?   Perhaps they were drinking this wine for months afterward? It is noticeable that Jesus does not just supply a jug or two of wine to try to tide them over. But there is an abundance in the provision. Jesus was not limited in what He could provide. His provision more than took care of the problem.

And so perhaps one of the spiritual lessons we might learn from this first sign is that God is not limited in His ability to solve our problems and meet our needs. He has an abundant storehouse, a storehouse so vast that it can supply all of our needs a thousand times over. We are more limited by our faith to accept the grace of God than we are by the nature of the grace of God itself.

3.   The scope of the grace of God:

Also we notice in the same vein that Jesus was taking an interest not in some life threatening illness, or some life and death situation. He was taking an interest in a situation where people thought they might die only of embarrassment. But Jesus and the grace of God is such that He is interested and concerned about us in the minutiae of life as well as the calamities of life. Just like a loving parent, He is concerned about the everyday matters of life as well as in the crises of life. It doesn't have to be a crisis before God is interested and concerned. He is as concerned about us on the football field and the supermarket as He is in the Intensive Care Unit.

There is a tendency for man to want to keep God at a distance and just bring Him out when the roof caves in or the bottom falls out of our lives. For many today, God is to be kept locked away in a glass case which will only be broken open in the event of emergency.

God's loving grace is extended to us in everyday living we don't need to exclude Him from everything but the great crises of life.

If we are to truly help our seeker after truth to engage with the text there are some things that we need to focus on. How do we encourage someone reading this passage perhaps for the first time to wrestle with the real issues?

Discussion Points:

1. What do we learn about Jesus from this miracle?

   What about the scope of the miracle? What does this tell us about the power and ability of Jesus? What does this miracle tell us about the character of Jesus? Were these people in a life or death situation? And yet Christ was concerned about their plight. He was interested in them and their problems even when they were not earth shattering or life threatening. What does this tell us about how God wants to be involved in our everyday lives and situations? What does this event tell us about the quality of God's solutions to our problems? Not only was the wine shortage solved but look at the quality of the solution. Look at the quantity of God's solution to man's problems. Did God just patch over the difficulty with a small amount to tide them over or was God's solution abundant and more than sufficient for their needs?

2. What were the effects of the miracle?

   We need to continually ask what the effect of these miracles were. Jesus never performed a miracle for His own benefit but it was always to answer a need in others. Ask the question. What were the effects of this miracle? Obviously some of the effects were physical and some were spiritual.

In the physical realm, a need was answered. They were in an enormously embarrassing situation. In that society they considered that they had a sacred duty to provide hospitality for their guests. And now the wine has run out. What an embarrassment! They wished the ground would open up and swallow them. But Jesus answered their physical need in a very abundant way. They had more wine than they knew what to do with. And that wine was of the finest quality. A physical need was supplied.

3. What are the spiritual imperatives we learn from this miracle?

Yes there was a spiritual dimension also. And this is suggested most strongly by v11. *He manifested His glory.* This was more than just being helpful. He was declaring something about Himself. He was demonstrating that He had power beyond anticipation or hope. Surely this must be the One who was promised. Surely this is Messiah who has come into our midst. This is what was spoken of in chapter one of John. *In the beginning was the Word and the Word was with God and the Word was God... and the Word became flesh and dwelt among us, and we have beheld His glory, glory as of the only Son from the Father.*

4. What was the effect on the disciples?

And the spiritual goes beyond that demonstration of power. For v11 states further that the effect of being in such close proximity to the miraculous power which is God, the disciples were led to believe in Him. In fact this was a process of faith which was to continue throughout His public ministry and the more they saw of this Jesus the more they were caused to have faith in Him. We might ask ...

• If you had been there, and seen these things, what would you have believed about this Jesus?

He did it to help the people who were in need… And He did it to build up the faith of His disciples. He was the God who came near. He did it to cause you to believe in Him also.

Remember at the conclusion of this study to thank the person for their time and express appreciation for the opportunity of opening the Word together with them. Indeed I usually express thanks to the person because every time I conduct a study it does me good to study the Word again. And I express in so many words that our study together has helped me and I hoped it has helped him/her also.

Chapter Six

The Second Sign: Healing at a Distance

IN THE LAST CHAPTER, WE began looking at the seven signs of John's gospel. We examined the first of the seven signs, which took place in Cana when Jesus visited the wedding feast. This is an event that we needed to share because it says some powerful things about Jesus and helps the seeker to come into contact with Jesus for the first time. It is an integral part of the story of the Redeemer and thus becomes an integral part of the story of redemption. And redemption must be seen and apprehended if we are to come to terms with who we are. It is part of our identity and without the story of redemption we shall ever be in an identity crisis.

The act of evangelism is one in which we labor to show Jesus to the world. In all of His glorious majesty, in all of His devoted service, we see Him through the things which He did. We see Him in the way that He treated people, helped people, healed people, saved people. This is the Jesus we all need to come to know. So there was something about the Jesus at the wedding feast in Cana that each one needs to see if we are to come to know Him. And in seeing Him we see the perfect image of the graciousness of God. We behold His glory, glory as of the only Son from the Father.

In this lesson we move to the closing verses of chapter four and we find Jesus co-incidentally in Cana once more. How marvelous it must have been to be a resident of the town of Cana and to see these signs of Jesus. How do you think you might have reacted to these things? Would you have been:

- Stoically unimpressed.
- Pleased at the entertainment value of it all.
- Persuaded to listen and follow Jesus yourself.

Naturally we might hope that all of us would fall into the last category. However we might be sure that there would have been some in the population of Cana who fell into each category.

There are some who say that if Jesus had lived today, He could have performed His miracles on live satellite link and been beamed to every country in the world, then everyone would believe in Him. And yet, strangely, you know, there would still be some who refused to believe. For faith ultimately is a matter of choice. Just as you today will have a choice as we examine this passage and think about the evidence of what Jesus did. You will choose whether to believe in Him and follow Him, or not.

Let us turn to the passage and read it carefully together. We must look at what happened and ask ourselves some important questions.

- What good did it do?
- What effect did it have on others?
- What does it say about Jesus?
- What does it mean for us?

> [46] *So he came again to Cana in Galilee, where he had made the water wine. And at Capernaum there was an official whose son was ill.* [47] *When he heard that Jesus had come from Judea to Galilee, he went and begged him to come down and heal his son, for he was at the point of death.* [48] *Jesus therefore said to him, "Unless you see signs and wonders you will not believe."* [49] *The official said to him, "Sir, come down before my child dies."* [50] *Jesus said to him, "Go; your son will live." The man believed the word that Jesus spoke to*

him and went his way. [51] As he was going down, his servants
met him and told him that his son was living. [52] So he asked
them the hour when he began to mend, and they said to
him, "Yesterday at the seventh hour the fever left him." [53]
The father knew that was the hour when Jesus had said to
him, "Your son will live"; and he himself believed, and all
his household. [54] This was now the second sign that Jesus did
when he had come from Judea to Galilee. Jn 4:46-54.

At the outset we must familiarize ourselves with the passage, think about it, pray about it, meditate upon it. We must eat, sleep and drink the passage until we have become so close to it we can see ourselves in the story. In this way we will allow the Scripture to speak to us, in order that we might speak to others of the wonderful grace of Jesus.

Jesus and the Nobleman

As we begin our consideration of this miracle, we should take note of the fine hymn in many hymn books based on this event. As we read we are perhaps reminded of the words of a lovely hymn *Come Down Lord*.

Come down Lord, my son is ill, wracked with fever the
live long day; He is life to me, if you will, drive death
away, drive death away. Lord do not come to my house,
I'm unworthy, speak and the promise is sealed. For when
your word O God is spoken, He shall be healed, he shall be
healed.

As we think about this event, let us notice what we learn from reading the text. Let us begin by noticing the chief character apart from Jesus in the story. We should note in passing that there is another similar miracle performed by Jesus which is recorded in Matthew chapter 8 and Luke chapter 7 where Jesus heals a centurion's servant. Although there are similarities, it is clear that this must be a similar but different miracle because there are significant details that are different in the two instances.

In one case the miracle took place in Capernaum and in the other it was in Cana. In one instance it was a centurion and in John it is a totally different kind of position held by the man. And in Matthew the man's servant is ill where here it is the man's son. So there are two different miracles. Now that we have that out of the way let us examine the miracle more closely.

1. The Man.

What can we see about the man? Firstly we notice that the man was an important man, a man of position and prestige. In one version he is referred to as "an official". Barclay calls him a courtier. The word used was *basilikos*. This is the word used for a royal official and hence a man of high standing in the court of Herod.

Get the ironical nature of this meeting. The royal official, came to see the village Carpenter.

Some time ago I read in my newspaper of the case of the young girl who was suffering from a dreadful disease, new variant CJD. She was taken from Britain to San Francisco for treatment because there was no effective treatment in this country. The doctors had told her parents she had at most twelve months to live and there was nothing that they could do. The parents heard about treatment on the internet and got agreement that they could take their daughter to America to receive new drug treatment for the disease and she has returned back home able to walk again with apparently a great reversal in the advancement of the disease.

If you were the parent how far would you be willing to go? If there was treatment in San Francisco or in Vladivostok, or Peking, would you get there? The answer is of course you would not care how much it cost, or how long it took but you would make sure that your son or your daughter got the treatment that they needed.

This man probably walked some considerable distance or rode on a donkey in order to bring his request before Jesus. According to Barclay's Daily Study Bible, the distance from Capernaum to Cana was of the order of twenty miles.[6] The lad is obviously too ill to make the journey. The father would have taken the better part of a whole day to

---

[6] Daily Study Bible, The Gospel of John Vol., p169 by William Barclay.

walk from Capernaum to Cana in order to seek the help of Jesus. He would gladly have walked twice or three times the distance if only Jesus would consent to help. Perhaps he imagined the Teacher telling him that he was too busy to make a detour of a couple of days journeying to his home to heal the boy and he might have to plead in order to save his son. But Jesus was to come up with a second plan. This was a plan which involved less time from Jesus, but infinitely more faith from the man.

Not only was the man not afraid of expending effort, but He was filled with a remarkable faith in the ability of Jesus to help. And he was not afraid of what people might say concerning him.

Can you imagine the things that would have been said? "You'll never guess what we just heard about one of the officials at the court of Herod. Left the king's court to go and consult a lunatic heretic from Nazareth of all places". No doubt he would have been a laughing stock at the court of Herod if it were known that he sought the help of Jesus. The court of Herod was not a place in which there was

- sympathy for,
- interest in,
- or respect for the ministry of Jesus.

Can you imagine what ridicule, or perhaps even danger the man was opening himself up to. He could have been laughed at, mocked, driven out of the court or even worse. But the man thought nothing about these things. He was consumed by a great need, a great need that only Jesus could satisfy. And he took that need to Jesus regardless of the cost.

If we want the help of Christ, there are times when we have to swallow our pride, and not care what any man might say or even do to us.

2. The command.

Next we should examine the command of Jesus to the man. The man is told to turn around and go home and accept that at the word of Jesus the boy would be healed.

It must have been hard for him to turn away and go home with Jesus' assurance that his little lad would live. It would have been easier if Jesus had told him that all he had to do was apply an ointment faithfully three times a day until the boy was cured or build an altar thirteen feet tall and 8 feet across. If Jesus had told him to do that he would have had something, a task to do. However in this case all he had to do was accept the word of Christ in faith. Perhaps we think of the example of Naaman in the Old Testament.

> *⁹ So Naaman came with his horses and chariots, and halted at the door of Elisha's house. ¹⁰ And Elisha sent a messenger to him, saying, "Go and wash in the Jordan seven times, and your flesh shall be restored, and you shall be clean." ¹¹ But Naaman was angry, and went away, saying, "Behold, I thought that he would surely come out to me, and stand, and call on the name of the LORD his God, and wave his hand over the place, and cure the leper. ¹² Are not Abana and Pharpar, the rivers of Damascus, better than all the waters of Israel? Could I not wash in them, and be clean?" So he turned and went away in a rage. ¹³ But his servants came near and said to him, "My father, if the prophet had commanded you to do some great thing, would you not have done it? How much rather, then, when he says to you, 'Wash, and be clean'?" ¹⁴ So he went down and dipped himself seven times in the Jordan, according to the word of the man of God; and his flesh was restored like the flesh of a little child, and he was clean. 2 Kings 5: 9-14.*

Naaman had to accept that by dipping in the Jordan seven times he would receive the blessing of God. If he substituted some other river he would not have been cleansed. If he had dipped six times and not seven he would not have been cleansed. He had to accept the instruction of God in faith and be cleansed.

This is a perfect analogy to our baptism. Some have stated in the past, I don't see why it is necessary to be baptized. I don't think that it should be necessary. But we have to accept the instruction of Jesus in faith and we shall in faith receive our cleansing just as Naaman did. So also with this man, in the passage in John's gospel. He had to accept the word of Christ in faith, turn around and walk home accepting that the miracle was done, even though he did not have evidence of it yet. What would you have done? Stay and argue? Or turn around and go home to accept the healing that the Savior offered? I wonder about that for myself. I can see myself staying and arguing and imploring Jesus to have a change of heart and agree to accompany me. What do you think would have been the result of this miracle on that household?

- No problems believing after this.
- No words of criticism would be allowed against Jesus in their presence
- A household of believers in Jesus?

Jesus and the Sign.

Let us turn now to look at Jesus and what this sign says about Him. This is significant because John with the aid of the Holy Spirit has selected this event as one of the seven out of the multitudes of miracles that Jesus performed. Why?

1. Compassion

First of all it is significant because we see in this the wonderful compassion of the Christ. Jesus based himself a lot of the time in Capernaum. Indeed one passage says that He was at home in Capernaum. i.e. there must have been a place there where He usually stayed. The man came from Capernaum. This may be the reason that the remarkable character of Jesus was known there. Whether He performed any miracles there previously may be debatable since this passage implied that this was only the second miracle He had performed in Galilee. But certainly the compassion of Christ seems to be anticipated in this passage. One thought in passing; I wonder if this is the home where Jesus stayed following this incident and if the home of this man was where Jesus would be made to feel at home in Capernaum.

Certainly this speaks to us loud and clear about the compassion of the Christ. In this passage, we are dealing with a caring Christ. We are still dealing with a caring Christ today. And when the bottom drops out of our world the way it dropped out of this man's world then we have to remember that we are still dealing with a Caring Christ.

- When no one else will help, Jesus will.
- When no one else can help, Jesus can.

2. Healing at a distance

Whenever you hear of so called healing miracles today, they seem to be more concerned with what some have called "faith healing". i.e. someone comes along to see a faith-healer and the person tells them they are cured and the more they think about it the more sure they are that yes they do appear to feel better. The healing seems to depend wholly on the faith of the recipient of the miracle and usually there is quite an amount of hocus-pocus and ceremony to assist the person to "feel healed."

Mostly also, the miracle is associated with some ill-defined non-visible form of illness. It does not deal with restoring an amputated limb, or bringing back to life someone who is dead and buried. Not the kind of miracles that we see Jesus performing in the gospel accounts. What do we see in this instance?

a) No hocus-pocus to assist faith:

Indeed we notice that the boy who was ill never heard Jesus speak, never saw Him, and Jesus never laid hands on him at any time. Indeed the boy was not in the same house, not even in the same town. The boy was 20 miles away, probably barely conscious and certainly not aware of Jesus' words, nor His actions, nor His promises.

b) This was a piece of remote healing. No medicines of any sort were applied.

Nor did anyone in the house where the boy lay ill and dying have any idea what was happening at that moment 20 miles away in Cana. The patient never received a touch, nor heard a word from Jesus the healer. The boy was unaware of the intervention of Jesus until it was effective. He did not display any faith, though his father did. There was no psychological trickery here. This was no psychological, or psychosomatic healing of an imaginary or psychological illness. The boy was dying and Jesus healed him, though he was never in his presence, never in the same house and never in the same town whilst he was suffering.

This is power!

Discussion Points:

What does this miracle mean for us today? What are we meant to conclude from it? Let us think about a couple of points.

1. Is He still the Compassionate Christ?

    When we are in the midst of trials and difficulties, He is still the One who cares. Some years ago I was in a discussion class and we asked every member of the class to close their eyes and imagine Jesus sitting in the circle. After a few moments we opened our eyes and we asked as many people who would, to share what they saw with their eyes closed. Some said he had long hair. One said that he was wearing blue jeans. But there was one recurring theme around the class. Several people mentioned his eyes and they said He had the kind of eyes that when you looked into them you just knew that He cared about you. Yes that is the Jesus we are dealing with.

2. Can we dare to trust His promises?

    We don't know if this official had seen any miracles at the
    hand of Jesus or not. But we do know that his faith was
    great. We know that he chose to believe in the promise of
    Jesus and journey home in faith.

    We need to have the same faith as this. When He
    promises us forgiveness of sins, we need to know that He
    is the Jesus who keeps His promises. When He promises
    His care and protection, we need to have the same faith
    that made this man in the story turn on his heel and begin
    the walk home. When He promises a heavenly home, that
    He has gone to prepare a place for us, we need to know
    that the promises of the Caring Christ are still as sure and
    certain as when Jesus said, *go on your way your son will live.*
    We know we can trust the promises of Christ.

    > *⁸Jesus Christ is the same yesterday and today
    > and for ever. Heb 13:8*

    He is eternal, He is the same. We can trust Him. He still
    does miraculous things in the lives of His followers.

3. What will the world think of me if I were to be a disciple
    of Jesus?

    One final thought is that we need to never mind what the
    world thinks about us. There is another's opinion which is
    far more important.

    The world thought Noah was crazy for building a big
    boat, and they were just plain wet for thinking that way.
    The world thought Abraham was crazy for leaving his
    home in Ur to go and live in tents, but he received a
    heavenly home instead.

    The world thought the disciples were crazy to leave
    their fishing business, their tax collecting business, their
    doctoring business to follow around on a mission for

the Master from Nazareth. But they brought the story of redemption to a dying world.

Let us dare to be disciples today. Jesus is calling disciples who will turn our city upside down, our world upside down for Him.

How can we assist others to truly engage with this text? The main weapon in our arsenal is simply questions. Questions make people think about what they have read. They make us think more deeply about the incident and what it can mean for us. And part of our preparation for teaching the truth of this great passage is to consider what questions we might employ to help this person we care about, this person whom we love in the Lord to truly engage with the text and meet Jesus there.

The questions are not high flown philosophical ones. The questions are not deep theological ones. Let me illustrate with some suggestions of mine. These are not the only questions. You might consider they are not even the best questions. Great! Now you are thinking in the right way. What are the best questions that will help draw someone into this marvelous narrative so that can start learning to appreciate Jesus more?

1. What do you think was going through the man's mind when he set out on his journey to Cana?

2. Do you think he rehearsed what he was going to say when he got there?

3. Why do you think he took the course of action that sent him on the long tiring journey to Cana?

4. What do you think went through the man's mind when Jesus told him to start on his return journey, that his son would be healed?

5. Why do you think the man did not argue with Jesus?

6. What effect do you think this incident had on the faith of the man?

7. What effect do you think this miracle had on the household of the man?

8. Do you think this family kept this story quiet or told it all over Capernaum?

Now add your own…

9.

10.

Chapter Seven

The Third Sign: The Man by the Pool

WE LOOKED AT THE FIRST two of the seven signs of Jesus recorded in John's gospel. The first sign was the water turned into wine and the second was the healing of the nobleman's son, a healing at a distance. Both recorded signs occurred in the city of Cana. Let us now turn our attention to another reading from the Scriptures and another sign:

> *[1] After this there was a feast of the Jews, and Jesus went up to Jerusalem. [2] Now there is in Jerusalem by the Sheep Gate a pool, in Hebrew called Beth-zatha, which has five porticoes. [3] In these lay a multitude of invalids, blind, lame, paralyzed. [5] One man was there, who had been ill for thirty-eight years. [6] When Jesus saw him and knew that he had been lying there a long time, he said to him, "Do you want to be healed?" [7] The sick man answered him, "Sir, I have no man to put me into the pool when the water is troubled, and while I am going another steps down before me." [8] Jesus said to him, "Rise, take up your pallet, and walk." [9] And at once the man was healed, and he took up his pallet and walked. Now that day was the Sabbath. [10] So the Jews said to the man who was cured, "It is the Sabbath, it is not lawful for you to carry your pallet." [11] But he answered them, "The man who healed*

*me said to me, 'Take up your pallet, and walk.'" [12] They
asked him, "Who is the man who said to you, 'Take up your
pallet, and walk'?" [13] Now the man who had been healed
did not know who it was, for Jesus had withdrawn, as there
was a crowd in the place. [14] Afterward, Jesus found him in
the temple, and said to him, "See, you are well! Sin no more,
that nothing worse befall you." [15] The man went away and
told the Jews that it was Jesus who had healed him. [16] And
this was why the Jews persecuted Jesus, because he did this
on the Sabbath. [17] But Jesus answered them, "My Father is
working still, and I am working." [18] This was why the Jews
sought all the more to kill him, because he not only broke
the Sabbath but also called God his Father, making himself
equal with God. Jn 5:1-17.*

A Notable Sign.

1. The Scene:

For this third sign we now switch our attention to the city of
Jerusalem. We are told that Jesus has visited Jerusalem for the feast. We
are not told exactly which feast this was, except we can assume that it
was one of the three great feasts during which Jews were obligated to
attend the temple. For those who lived within 20 miles of Jerusalem,
they were legally obliged to attend. But others traveled many long
miles to make sure that they were present. The great three were
Passover, Pentecost and Tabernacles. It does not really matter which of
the three this is. Back in chapter two, Jesus had attended Jerusalem for
the Feast of Passover, and again in chapter six He is in Jerusalem for
the Passover. Some commentators have now pieced this together and
conclude that there are three Passovers mentioned during the public
ministry of Jesus in John's gospel account. Indeed, were it not for the
gospel of John, we could not tell that the ministry of Jesus lasted for
three years.

The events of this miracle occur at one of the pools in Jerusalem.
Some Bibles call it the Pool of Bethesda (which means "House of
Mercy") and some Bibles call it the Pool of Bethzatha" (which means

"House of Olives"). Josephus tells us that there was a part of Jerusalem which was called Bethzatha, so perhaps the Pool of Bethesda was in the quarter of the city called Bethzatha.

The word for pool used is a word which is based on the verb "to dive", and this implies that this was no mere paddling pool but something large enough to swim in. Another interesting piece of background information is we are told that the pool was surrounded by 5 porticoes. Hence the pool had around it a covered area in which the sick and the infirm could be protected from the weather, shaded from the heat of the sun whilst they waited to receive the help they thought was possible here.

2. The Angel of the Pool:

Beneath the pool, there was a subterranean stream which fed it. You will note that in most Bibles, v4 is omitted altogether because it is not in the best manuscripts. It is in v4 that the addition was made in ancient times which reflected the beliefs of the people at that time. They believed that the waters were troubled by an angel and only those who were in the pool first could receive a remarkable healing as a result of being in first when the angel stirred the waters. It is clear that this is what the people believed and this is why the sick and infirm gathered by the pool.

We might wonder why people adopted this belief. Was there an angel who troubled the waters? Were there healing miracles caused by the angel's intervention. Barnes has an interesting suggestion. The truth may well be that at different times the stream put forth an unusual quantity of water which caused the water level in the pool to rise suddenly. When this happened the constituents of the water might well have been enriched by particular minerals and trace elements which were medicinally quite beneficial for helping people with certain conditions. In the same way that there are spas in different parts of the world which people flock to and seem to be helped, so also here. But because some people were helped and many more found no difference in their conditions, the people interpreted this by saying that it was only the people who were first in the pool that were helped. This may have come from the fact that if you were in the pool at the time when the beneficial waters came through then you were more likely to be helped than if you waited for the water level to go back down and the less beneficial waters were all that were left in the pool.

And so the hopeful gathered around the pool hoping to be first into the water to be helped by the "angel of the pool of mercy."

3. Jesus and the Law:

It is necessary for us to make a comment on the relationship between Jesus and the Law because of the criticism of the Jewish leaders when they witnessed the events at the pool of Bethesda.

This is a sad comment on the Jewish leaders when you think about it. They saw a man who was a hopeless cripple who at the word of Jesus was completely cured and able to walk. Thirty-eight years he had suffered from this debilitating condition. He had lain on his pallet and unable to walk. Now the man is walking about and carrying his bed. And the only thing the Jewish leaders wanted to talk about was whether the man was breaking the law in carrying his bed. They saw this a flagrant offence against the Sabbath laws.

To carry burdens on the Sabbath day was forbidden by the Old Testament.

> *[21] Thus says the LORD: Take heed for the sake of your lives, and do not bear a burden on the Sabbath day or bring it in by the gates of Jerusalem. Jer 17:21.*

> *[15] In those days I saw in Judah men treading wine presses on the Sabbath, and bringing in heaps of grain and loading them on asses; and also wine, grapes, figs, and all kinds of burdens, which they brought into Jerusalem on the Sabbath day; and I warned them on the day when they sold food. Neh 13:15.*

> *[8] "Remember the Sabbath day, to keep it holy. [9] Six days you shall labor, and do all your work; [10] but the seventh day is a Sabbath to the LORD your God; in it you shall not do any work, you, or your son, or your daughter, your manservant, or your maidservant, or your cattle, or the sojourner who is within your gates; [11] for in six days the LORD made heaven*

and earth, the sea, and all that is in them, and rested the
seventh day; therefore the LORD *blessed the Sabbath day and*
hallowed it.
Ex 20:8-11.

These were the passages which supported the contention of the
Jewish leaders that Jesus had encouraged the man to break the Old
Testament Law. But there are other things we need to bear in mind
when we think about this:

a. Jesus wanted them to know that He was Lord of the
    Sabbath.

    When we look at what Jesus says in response to their
    criticism. The answer of Jesus was to say that God must be
    breaking the Sabbath too! He is still working. The world is
    still spinning on its axis. Does God stop looking after His
    people because it is the Sabbath? No! And since God is
    still working then so am I!

b. Further we note that these passages do not condemn the
    man for doing what Jesus told him to do. The passages
    forbade the Jews from carrying on work for personal gain
    on the Sabbath. It was to be a special day, a day in which
    they devoted themselves to God. Jesus was doing the work
    of God in healing the man. There was no conflict with the
    Law in this. And carrying a burden was about transporting
    goods for sale around; it was about bringing in produce;
    it was about carrying on as if the Sabbath was no different
    from any other day. The man was a poor man and Jesus
    was instructing him to take care of his property. Should he
    leave his bed at this public place and not have it with him
    any more?

c. The Jews had extended their regulations far beyond what
    the law intended. They were permitted to pull an animal
    out of a ditch on the Sabbath rather than let it die. But
    apparently they did not extend the same mercy towards
    this man who lay by the pool of mercy.

d. Jesus was having nothing to do with this kind of nonsense and so He has no compunction in flouting the additional regulations, man had burdened the Jews with. They had in this instance totally lost touch with what the Law required of them. Look at what Jesus had to say about this, these words recorded by Matthew in his gospel account.

¹ Then Pharisees and scribes came to Jesus from Jerusalem and said, ² "Why do your disciples transgress the tradition of the elders? For they do not wash their hands when they eat." ³ He answered them, "And why do you transgress the commandment of God for the sake of your tradition? ⁴ For God commanded, 'Honor your father and your mother,' and, 'He who speaks evil of father or mother, let him surely die.' ⁵ But you say, 'If any one tells his father or his mother, What you would have gained from me is given to God, he need not honor his father.' ⁶ So, for the sake of your tradition, you have made void the word of God. ⁷ You hypocrites! Well did Isaiah prophesy of you, when he said: ⁸ 'This people honors me with their lips, but their heart is far from me; ⁹ in vain do they worship me, teaching as doctrines the precepts of men.'" Mt 15:1-9.

This sign again reminds us of the compassion of Jesus in reaching out to this poor man by the Pool of Bethesda. We need to consider the implications of this particular miracle and what it means for us today.

Spiritual Lessons from a Notable Sign.

Let us look at some implications of this event.

1. The Right of the Healer to Speak.

We notice that the Jews wanted to know who it was that had instructed the man to carry his bed. The man is happy to tell them that it was the man Jesus who had told him. After all, if Jesus could do this remarkable healing on the basis of His spoken word, then why should he not instruct us about matters of the Law? The point is a vital one and perhaps one of the main reasons for this being in our Bibles.

> *5 And when Jesus saw their faith, he said to the paralytic, "My son, your sins are forgiven." 6 Now some of the scribes were sitting there, questioning in their hearts, 7 "Why does this man speak thus? It is blasphemy! Who can forgive sins but God alone?" 8 And immediately Jesus, perceiving in his spirit that they thus questioned within themselves, said to them, "Why do you question thus in your hearts? 9 Which is easier, to say to the paralytic, 'Your sins are forgiven,' or to say, 'Rise, take up your pallet and walk'? 10 But that you may know that the Son of man has authority on earth to forgive sins"—he said to the paralytic— 11 "I say to you, rise, take up your pallet and go home." 12 And he rose, and immediately took up the pallet and went out before them all; so that they were all amazed and glorified God, saying, "We never saw anything like this!" Mk 2:5-12.*

If Jesus could speak and the man with infirmity for 38 years could pick up his bed and walk, then He surely has the right to interpret the Law for us and show us the proper understanding of things spiritual and things eternal.

If Jesus could bring the paralyzed man up from his bed and back into the land of the living, then He has the right to forgive sins too. This miracle of Jesus says something very significant to us in the here and now. Jesus is the one with the right to speak to us, to lead us spiritually, to guide us eternally, to bring us into right paths.

2.   The Identity of the Healer Established:

Further we see how this fits into the overall plan of John. Because He heals when no one else could heal, because He displays this power that no one else could display then it establishes who He is!

¹⁷ But Jesus answered them, "My Father is working still, and I am working." ¹⁸ This was why the Jews sought all the more to kill him, because he not only broke the Sabbath but also called God his Father, making himself equal with God.

The Jews understood only too clearly the implications of what Jesus meant when He referred to God as His Father! He was speaking of a very unique relationship which identified Jesus as of the same substance as God, as eternal as God is eternal, as powerful as God is powerful, as all-knowing as God is all-knowing. So they sought to kill Him because He made himself equal with God.

The Experience of the Sufferer.

As we look at the experience of the infirm man what do we see?

Do you want to be healed? Jesus starts with the question, "Do you want to be healed?" This may sound like a strange question but it is not. He may have lain there so long that he has lost all hope of ever being helped and he has just learned to accept his limitations. But we note that the man did want to be helped. He still lived in hope of being helped.

And this reflects our circumstances today. We live with the limitations of sin in our lives. It hampers us. It stops us from living full spiritual lives. It leaves us spiritually crippled.

And Jesus still comes and asks the question, "do you want to be healed?" If you are perceptive enough, then you see that you are in that position today. You need to be like this man and still want passionately to be healed of the disease of sin in your soul.

Accept the impossible. We need like this man to be ready to accept the impossible. Note that Jesus told him to stand up and pick up his bed. He could have said, *I can't stand up. I can't pick up my bed. I can't walk. Don't talk romantic. These are the things which are impossible for me that is why I need your help.*

And if he had thought that way he would have remained on his pallet and never walked. Jesus calls upon us to believe in Him. Believe that He can change everything. He can make us walk spiritually. He can take us, those who are lame and infirm spiritually and have us walking and leaping and jumping in His service. All we have to do is to believe Him. We might be holding back and saying to ourselves, "I don't think I can live the Christian life. I don't think I can truly be a disciple of Jesus". Dare to believe the impossible . For with Jesus, the impossible becomes commonplace.

You see your life could have gone in a totally different direction. You could be a totally different person if it were not for your commitment to God. Think about this, what sort of person would I be if I had not become a Christian? Or if I am at the crossroads in life, what sort of person will I become if I choose not to become a Christian?

If the world were to take the ruling hand in your life instead of the Savior, what sort of person would you be? You can choose today to stay on your pallet as the spiritual cripple and not learn to walk in His way. But if you are smart, you will grasp what He offers you and stand up and walk.

Discussion:

1. What does this miracle tell us about the power of Jesus?

2. What does this miracle teach us about the nature of Jesus?

3. What does this miracle teach us about the authority of Jesus?

4. What does this miracle have to do with us today?

5. If you had been there, how would you describe this when interviewed by the local TV station afterward?

6. Does this miracle make a spiritual point?

7. In the text what reactions do you see to Jesus?

    a. Attack Him! Kill Him! (v17) He broke our traditions. He is lawless. We shall seek to kill Him.

b.   Honor Him!

²² The Father judges no one, but has given all judgment to the Son, ²³ that all may honor the Son, even as they honor the Father. He who does not honor the Son does not honor the Father who sent him.

c.   Believe Him!

²⁴ Truly, truly, I say to you, he who hears my word and believes him who sent me, has eternal life; he does not come into judgment, but has passed from death to life.

What is our reaction to Jesus today? We need to believe in Him with all of our heart. Believe Him and believe in Him! Will you? Accept Him! Accept and obey the Gospel for it is this He calls you to.

Chapter Eight

The Fourth Sign: The Feeding of a Multitude

I N THIS CHAPTER WE COME to the fourth of the signs, which is the Feeding of the 5000. For this we shall turn to John ch 6 for our reading.

> *¹ After this Jesus went to the other side of the Sea of Galilee, which is the Sea of Tiberias. ² And a multitude followed him, because they saw the signs which he did on those who were diseased. ³ Jesus went up on the mountain, and there sat down with his disciples. ⁴ Now the Passover, the feast of the Jews, was at hand. ⁵ Lifting up his eyes, then, and seeing that a multitude was coming to him, Jesus said to Philip, "How are we to buy bread, so that these people may eat?" ⁶ This he said to test him, for he himself knew what he would do. ⁷ Philip answered him, "Two hundred denarii would not buy enough bread for each of them to get a little." ⁸ One of his disciples, Andrew, Simon Peter's brother, said to him, ⁹ "There is a lad here who has five barley loaves and two fish; but what are they among so many?" ¹⁰ Jesus said, "Make the people sit down." Now there was much grass in the place; so the men sat down, in number about five thousand. ¹¹ Jesus then took the loaves, and when he had given thanks, he distributed them to those who were seated; so also the fish, as*

*much as they wanted. [12] And when they had eaten their fill,
he told his disciples, "Gather up the fragments left over, that
nothing may be lost." [13] So they gathered them up and filled
twelve baskets with fragments from the five barley loaves,
left by those who had eaten. [14] When the people saw the sign
which he had done, they said, "This is indeed the prophet
who is to come into the world!" John 6:1-14.*

Now we must turn our attention towards the caring Christ who gave and kept on giving. Isn't it interesting that Jesus did not decide to instigate His new kingdom by blowing Himself up and taking as many Romans as possible with Him? He was no suicide bomber. He just kept on giving Himself and bringing people to faith and hence causing countless internal revolutions in the hearts of men and women. Every day, and in every township, and in every circumstance in life, Jesus caused revolution in the hearts of men and women.

For Christianity is not a political movement, it is a spiritual movement. It does not exist to make political statements or adopt political stances, but it exists to save and to change people from the inside out and every time it does that, it makes the world a better place.

Let us notice the main points of this wonderful passage in John 6. It will be good for us to notice some introductory matters to begin with.

Some introductory matters:

1. Geographical matters:

There were times when Jesus desired to withdraw away from the crowds. He was under continuous strain with the needs of so many day after day. The sick and the infirm cried out for healing and He could leave no request unmet. The hopeless and faithless needed to see God and they saw God in Him. The confused and the ignorant needed to know of God's love for them, and He would not hold back in his message of hope. The Kingdom was coming, after so many generations of waiting now was the time for Messiah to come. The King was coming to be enthroned. The message of the prophets was now coming to fruition. As He had proclaimed at the synagogue in

Nazareth, when He read from the prophet Isaiah and testified, *"This is now fulfilled in your hearing!"*

Now He needed time for prayer, He needed rest, He needed solitude. And so He got in a boat and crossed the Sea of Galilee at the Northern end of the great lake. And on this occasion it was probably wise for Him to withdraw in case the final confrontation with the authorities was brought on too quickly for it was not the time for His final confrontation. He had much teaching to do before He was taken away from them.

From Capernaum to the other side of the Sea of Galilee was a distance of some four miles. So he set sail for a relatively short crossing across the Sea. You can see in any map in your Bible or Bible atlas where Capernaum was and on the other side of the lake a place called Bethsaida-Julias. It was easy to see the direction in which the boat was traveling and the crowds decided to follow Jesus by walking round the northern shore of the lake. The River Jordan flowed into the lake there, and two miles up the Jordan there was a ford where people could cross the Jordan. Near the ford there was a village called Bethsaida Julias, and it was for that place that Jesus was heading.

> *[10] On their return the apostles told him what they had done. And he took them and withdrew apart to a city called Bethsaida.   Lke 9:10*

Near Bethsaida Julias, almost on the lakeside there was a little plain where the grass always grows. Its name was El-Batiyah and it was to be the scene of this wondrous happening.

2.   Practical Matters:

Notice the practical matters that Jesus is dealing with. The crowd were moved to follow Jesus around the lake, not really out of the highest of all motives. It was not that they were His devoted followers who were giving up everything to follow after Him. It was not that they even were enthralled by His teachings and this drove them to abandon everything to listen more to the teachings of the Master.

However the text makes it clear that they had followed after Jesus because they were amazed at the things which He did. The signs were amazing. This was the greatest show in town! And they wanted to see more. They had witnessed some miraculous healings and they wanted to see more.

We are told that the Feast of Passover was near and there would have been even bigger crowds on the roads at that time. Quite possibly many were already on route to Jerusalem in order to celebrate the feast. In fact many Jews refrained from traveling through the region of the Samaritans and this would have been in their direct path of going south to Jerusalem. And so they would have chosen to cross the Jordan at this point at Bethsaida Julias and travel down East of the Jordan to avoid the region of the Samaritans.

However as Jesus looked at the crowd, we wonder for a moment what went through His mind. If it had been me, I probably would have been frustrated or even angry. Did I not get in the boat to get away from you folks for a little while? Can I not have a day off? Is there nowhere to hide from this seething mass of humanity?

And yet as we see Jesus looking at the crowd He looks at them through different eyes. He sees the crowd coming from a distance and He asks Philip a question.

Where can we buy enough bread to feed all these people?

Why did Jesus ask the question? Did He not know? It is clear from the text He knew exactly what He was going to do and yet He asked the question in order to have an impact on Philip and the rest of the apostles. Philip lifts up his eyes and looks at the vast crowd advancing on them.

Six months wages would not feed this lot!

And of course he is right. It says later in the text that the number of the men was 5000. This did not include the women and children who we imagine would need to eat also. Could there have been 10,000 or 12,000 people in this vast crowd? Where could we get enough bread that these people might eat? There were two problems-

a. Where could we get enough bread? When we had a VBS one summer I took an order to Macdonald's for meals for around 50 people and if we had enough money then there was no real problem getting enough for the 50 people to be fed. And if there were more, then I think we could have found a catering firm in the yellow pages which could have come up with enough food to feed a large number of people. Near the village of Bethsaida-Julias around 28 AD where, just where could you buy enough food to feed 12,000 people? The problem was a logistical nightmare.

b. Secondly Philip homes in on another aspect of the practical problem. Six months wages would not be enough to deal with this problem. (Some modern translations suggest eight months wages here.) Suppose we said that a man's wages were £12,000, for the sake of round figures. Then we notice what is being said here is Lord we would need about £6000 (about $12,000), about 50 pence (or $1) a head just for everyone to get a bit of bread to eat. Those figures seem about right don't they? If you were to make everyone just one sandwich then these are the kind of figures you would be talking about.

So there were two large logistical problems to be dealt with in the miracle that Jesus performed. These problems are so immense that it is difficult to see how they could be overcome. With the best will in the world, where could you find a baker who could undertake that kind of job with no notice. Perhaps an army of bakers might be able to produce something given a few days notice. But the enormity of this need is so great that Philip could see nothing but problems.

Aspects of the Miracle Itself!

1. The Meal:

The first thing I want to draw attention to is the nature of the raw materials. We are told that it was five loaves and two fishes.

This conjures up pictures in our head which are quite misleading. In my mind I see a couple of huge salmon and five sliced loaves. And although this would not be much in the face of 12,000 people perhaps you could feed thirty or forty people something with such a supply. My wife tells me that you get eighteen slices of bread in a standard loaf sold in our supermarkets. If so you can get nine sandwiches out of a loaf. That is, if the kind of loaves in this story were the same as the kind of loaves we buy in our supermarket today.

However, this is not the case. What would the small boy have been doing with enough food for 50 people? This was the little boy's meal, or at most, his family's meal. Barley bread was the cheapest of all bread and was held in contempt. It was the bread of the very poor. They were probably more like the bread rolls we might be able to buy today. And the fish were probably salted fish. There were small fish pulled from the waters of the Sea of Galilee which were no bigger than sardines. They were salted and transported all over the Roman Empire. In those days anyone not living on the shores of the Sea would have regarded fresh fish as a great luxury.

So the raw materials that Jesus used for the miracle were a few rolls and a couple of sardines.

2. Andrew the Introducer:

It is an amazing fact that whenever you see Andrew in the New Testament he is almost always introducing people to Jesus. There are thirteen mentions of his name in the New Testament (some of these just in lists of the apostles), but whenever it says something about Andrew and what he did or said, it was about bringing people to Jesus.

Check this out. Let us notice one or two of these passages concerning the apostle Andrew and see what it says about him.

> [40] *One of the two who heard John speak, and followed him, was Andrew, Simon Peter's brother.* [41] *He first found his brother Simon, and said to him, "We have found the Messiah" (which means Christ).* [42] *He brought him to Jesus. Jesus looked at him, and said, "So you are Simon the son of*

John? You shall be called Cephas" (which means Peter). Jn 1:40-42.

⁸ One of his disciples, Andrew, Simon Peter's brother, said to him, ⁹ "There is a lad here who has five barley loaves and two fish; but what are they among so many?" Jn 6: 8-9.

²⁰ Now among those who went up to worship at the feast were some Greeks. ²¹ So these came to Philip, who was from Bethsaida in Galilee, and said to him, "Sir, we wish to see Jesus." ²² Philip went and told Andrew; Andrew went with Philip and they told Jesus. Jn 12:20-22.

Perhaps we need to be a little more like Andrew.

3. The Scale of the Miracle:

Sometimes if you are at a party or celebration of some kind and you notice that the food is not just as plentiful as it might be then you might take a very modest amount and make do with that and pretend that you have had enough! Here was a situation where 12000 people have to be fed by an ancient village with the only resources being a few rolls and a couple of sardines.

And yet the text here says that they were "filled". The word used is *chortazesthai*. And this word was used originally for the feeding of animals with fodder. In those instances where it was used of people it meant that they were glutted, sated, fed to fullness.

My wife's grandfather had a saying if you fed him a big meal he would lean back in his chair and say, "I am CFRB". And you could tell he just wanted you to ask what that meant and he would be pleased to tell you he was Crammed Full and Ready to Bust.

Such was the scale of this miracle that this vast crowd of people had not just politely nibbled at food on offer but were *CFRB* and could eat no more. And what is more, when they gathered up the fragments of what was left over, there were 12 baskets full of fragments left over!

This is telling us something about the ability of Jesus to deal with problems in life. Even when the need is humongous, even when the need is totally overwhelming like the need to feed these 12,000 people, the ability of Jesus makes the need pale into insignificance. There really is no need that He cannot deal with and deal with in such an abundant way that we wonder why did we doubt at all! Like Philip and like Andrew we needed to learn to trust in the ability of Jesus to deal with things in a superabundant way!

Conclusion:

I want us to notice what we can learn from the miracle from looking at three of the characters in the story.

Philip

Firstly we see Philip. Philip was the man who looked at the situation and said, the situation is hopeless, there is nothing that can be done. And there are times when perhaps we look at our situation and we think that too. But Jesus is patient with Philip so that Philip could learn that there was much that could be done when Jesus was on the scene. And so also with us. Perhaps there are times when we look at our situation and we say we are a small church, and it is a large city. Nationally, we are a small church and Britain has so many millions of people. We are small in resources and how can we really carry out the task. And yet like Philip there are things we need to learn.

1. One person and God is a majority! It is never hopeless when God is involved in our side.

2. Christ left the great commission to reach the whole world with 12 men in a tucked-away occupied nation in Palestine. What an impossible task! May as well give up! No listen....

[18] And Jesus came and said to them, "All authority in heaven and on earth has been given to me. [19] Go therefore and make disciples of all nations, baptizing them in the name of the Father and of the Son and of the Holy Spirit, [20] teaching

> *them to observe all that I have commanded you; and lo, I*
> *am with you always, to the close of the age." Mt 28:18-20*

3. And how are we to reach the whole of our city, the whole
   of our nation, the whole of the world with the gospel? The
   answer is one at a time! All we need to do is to start with
   our own household, start with our neighbors and speak to
   them one at a time. We will be amazed at how the power
   of the Gospel will reach people and each new person that
   is reached will in turn reach out to others till it snowballs
   as it did in New Testament times.

Andrew

Let's now turn to Andrew who figures mightily in the story!
Andrew couldn't solve the problem. He couldn't feed 12,000 people.
But he did what he could. He brought the small boy to Jesus. Without
knowing what would happen by just doing this very small thing, he
bought the boy to Jesus and Jesus solved the problem! We can't save
the city. And Jesus does not expect us to. But he says, be an Andrew
and bring a small boy to me. Bring a young girl to me and just watch
what I can do with the power of the gospel.

Who knows what great things might come out of our desire to
teach children in mid week Bible study evenings, or Sunday school
sessions. What small boys or girls will be brought to Jesus as a result
and what marvelous things will happen as a result.

We need your help to teach, to distribute leaflets, to invite people
to come along, to tell people good news and invite them to "come and
see", and then stand back to let Jesus do His wonders.

The Boy

The boy did not have much to offer. It was not the best of food.
There wasn't much of it. But the important thing was that he offered
everything that he had.

Sometimes we might feel a little like that. What do I have to offer
God? I am not a great speaker, I am not a great singer, I don't look

attractive like some film star, and I don't have a great education. But look at this boy and what Jesus was able to do with him!

If, just as we are, we would lay ourselves on the altar of service, then there is no limit to what Jesus can do with us. One preacher put it this way....

It's not so much ability as availability that counts!

Discussion Points:

1. What does this incident tell us about Jesus?

2. What does this incident tell us about Jesus and the impossible?

3. What does this incident teach us about the resources at the disposal of Jesus?

4. What does this incident teach us about the compassion of the Christ?

5. Imagine yourself as one of the disciples of Jesus involved in the distribution process. What do you think you saw as you carried the food around?

6. What impact do you think this had on the faith of the disciples?

7. Imagine yourself as a member of the multitude. Do you think you understood what was happening? (Look at v14).

8. What impact do you think this had on the faith of the multitude?

9. What impact does this have on your faith?

Chapter Nine

The Fifth Sign: Walking on Water

IN OUR STUDY OF JOHN'S gospel we come in this chapter to the fifth of the signs. It is interesting to note in passing that some of the signs seem to be linked to the "I AM" statements of the gospel account too.

e.g.

Sign	I AM
Feeding of 5000 (Jn 6)	I AM the Bread of Life. (Jn 6)
Healing of the Blind Man (Jn 9)	I AM the Light of the World. (Jn 8)
Raising of Lazarus (Jn 11)	I AM the Resurrection and the Life (Jn 11)

It is almost as if the signs illustrated perfectly the important sayings that Jesus wanted us to wrestle with and understand. This brings us back to our original premise that these signs were the ones the Holy Spirit thought were sufficient to point to Jesus as Son of God! He is the Bread of Life and we see Him miraculously feeding the great multitude. He is the Light of the World and we see Him bringing sight to the man born blind and living in darkness. He is the Resurrection and the Life and we see Him calling dead Lazarus from the grave. And these miraculous signs illustrate the great spiritual truths concerning this Jesus. These are dependable things. We can take these to the bank.

Let us turn to the sign we wish to consider in this chapter. We turn to John chapter six once again and look at events which immediately followed the miracle of Jesus feeding the great multitude. We are going to notice the response of the great multitude to the previous miracle and want to draw some conclusions from that as well as looking at the miracle that Jesus performed on this occasion:

> *[15] Perceiving then that they were about to come and take him by force to make him king, Jesus withdrew again to the mountain by himself. [16] When evening came, his disciples went down to the sea, [17] got into a boat, and started across the sea to Capernaum-um. It was now dark, and Jesus had not yet come to them. [18] The sea rose because a strong wind was blowing. [19] When they had rowed about three or four miles, they saw Jesus walking on the sea and drawing near to the boat. They were frightened, [20] but he said to them, "It is I; do not be afraid." [21] Then they were glad to take him into the boat, and immediately the boat was at the land to which they were going. Jn 6:15-21.*

We see a remarkable event that had a profound effect on the disciples, and John who writes this tells us an eyewitness account of what happened.

In order to help us with our understanding of the event and to prevent some serious misunderstandings from some commentators we have to read the parallel accounts carefully to piece the picture together. Let us look at the two other accounts of the same incident, which give us further information about what actually happened.

> *[22] Immediately he made the disciples get into the boat and go on ahead to the other side, while he dismissed the crowds. [23] And after he had dismissed the crowds, he went up the mountain by himself to pray. When evening came, he was there alone, [24] but by this time the boat, battered by the waves, was far from the land, for the wind was against them. [25] And early in the morning he came walking toward them on the sea. [26] But when the disciples saw him walking*

on the sea, they were terrified, saying, "It is a ghost!" And they cried out in fear. [27] But immediately Jesus spoke to them and said, "Take heart, it is I; do not be afraid."
[28] Peter answered him, "Lord, if it is you, command me to come to you on the water." [29] He said, "Come." So Peter got out of the boat, started walking on the water, and came toward Jesus. [30] But when he noticed the strong wind, he became frightened, and beginning to sink, he cried out, "Lord, save me!" [31] Jesus immediately reached out his hand and caught him, saying to him, "You of little faith, why did you doubt?" [32] When they got into the boat, the wind ceased. [33] And those in the boat worshiped him, saying, "Truly you are the Son of God." Mt 14:22-33.

[45] Immediately he made his disciples get into the boat and go before him to the other side, to Bethsaida, while he dismissed the crowd. [46] And after he had taken leave of them, he went up on the mountain to pray. [47] And when evening came, the boat was out on the sea, and he was alone on the land. [48] And he saw that they were making headway painfully, for the wind was against them. And about the fourth watch of the night he came to them, walking on the sea. He meant to pass by them, [49] but when they saw him walking on the sea they thought it was a ghost, and cried out; [50] for they all saw him, and were terrified. But immediately he spoke to them and said, "Take heart, it is I; have no fear." [51] And he got into the boat with them and the wind ceased. And they were utterly astounded, [52] for they did not understand about the loaves, but their hearts were hardened. Mk 6:45-52.

Let us note some important points from these readings from the New Testament. Surely there are some vital points we can learn from this incident.

The Actions of Jesus.

We must look carefully at what Jesus did. Then we want to move on to look at the effect of what Jesus did.

In the last chapter we saw Jesus having compassion on the crowds and feeding them using the small boy's lunch to feed up to 12,000 people. And then gathering up 12 baskets full of leftovers. We must look back at v 14-15

> *14 When the people saw the sign which he had done, they said, "This is indeed the prophet who is to come into the world!" 15 Perceiving then that they were about to come and take him by force to make him king, Jesus withdrew again to the mountain by himself.*

The feeding of the multitude had a dramatic effect on the crowd. This is indeed the prophet! Moses had predicted centuries before that from amongst their own nation would arise a great prophet. He was speaking of the Messiah who was to come. And they had been waiting on His coming for hundreds of years. Now when they saw the miracle with the bread and the fishes they proclaimed that this is the prophet. Messiah has come. And we see in v15 that they were going to come and make Him king by force and this was not what Jesus had come to do. He was later to proclaim, "My kingdom is not of this world".

Jesus knew very well that His ministry was on a collision course with the Jewish authorities, a course which would one day result in His death. But He also knew that the time for the ultimate collision was not now! So He withdrew quietly and allowed the disciples to disperse the crowd and to go without Him back across the sea to Capernaum. Mark in his account comments that He had sent them on ahead (Mk 6:45). He had gone to Bethsaida Julias in the first place for a quiet time of prayer and contemplation away from the crowds and now He withdrew to go up on the mountain to pray. He has ensured that the disciples also are removed from the inflamed passions of the crowd and their political aspirations by sending them ahead by boat instead of just waiting around for the Master to return.

In the early evening, the disciples set out without Him to cross back across to Capernaum to await Him there. Meanwhile up on the mountain Jesus has a view of the lake and can see that His disciples are caught in a sudden storm and are struggling to make headway against the wind. The language suggests that the sea was rising more and more as time when on. The scripture reports that a great wind was blowing.

- Matthew writes that the boat was distressed by the waves. (RSV battered by the waves).
- Mark writes that the disciples were distressed by the rowing. (RSV making headway painfully).

They had only traveled between three and four miles but that had taken them most of the night. The other evangelists mention the time when Jesus came to the boat was about the fourth watch of the night. i.e. it was between 3 and 6am when He came towards them in the boat. They had left in the early evening between 6 and 9pm. No wonder Mark comments that they were distressed by the rowing. They had been rowing most of the night and were having great difficulty making headway.

We don't know exactly how close they were to arriving at Capernaum and it is safe to conclude that in the dark, and in the midst of the storm neither did the disciples know. It was one of the situations where you had to be holding an oar in the boat before you knew just how bad it felt or how dangerous or how disorienting.

Just how spectacular would it have appeared from inside that boat to see Jesus walking across a sea that they could barely keep the boat afloat on!

- John says simply that when the disciples saw Jesus walking on the water they were frightened.
- Matthew and Mark both say they thought it was a ghost and they cried out for fear!
- But Jesus offers words of comfort… *It is I! Don't be afraid!*

Only Matthew tells the story of Peter getting out of the boat at the instruction of Jesus. John comments only that they were willing to take Him into the boat. I should think that they were!

John records a strange part of the miracle that the others do not mention!

> *Then they were glad to take him into the boat, and immediately the boat was at the land to which they were going.*

Not only did He walk on water, but also He calmed the storm, and He transported the boat instantaneously to its destination at the shore. Does this seem far-fetched to some? No more than calming the storm, and no more than walking on water. The one who walked on water was perfectly capable of all three miraculous actions.

Struggling Disciples: How Big is Your Jesus?

The closing statements of the accounts are worthy of our attention. Mark's account notes…

> *And they were utterly astounded, [52] for they did not understand about the loaves, but their hearts were hardened.*

The disciples were astounded at what Jesus had done… three miracles in one. And it was clear that they were unclear about the miracle with the loaves and fishes. They had been sent round distributing and collecting and even they were unsure about what exactly had been done. How could such a miracle be possible? And now miracle upon miracle we see Jesus adding to His original sign. Sometimes we think that the disciples were there so they would understand fully. But they were still wrestling with the miraculous things they were seeing with their own eyes and trying to figure out the implications of it all.

> [32] *When they got into the boat, the wind ceased.* [33] *And those in the boat worshiped him, saying, "Truly you are the Son of God." Mt 14:32-33.*

I suppose ultimately the conclusion was inescapable. When the disciples considered all that their eyes had seen, there was only one conclusion. This is Messiah! This is the Christ! This is the Son of God. And John wrote his gospel that we too might reach the same conclusion.

It was an interesting experience studying for this lesson. I had started my study with Barclay and felt very strange about the conclusions he arrived at. When I was a boy I used to organize newspaper deliveries in an area on the South Side of Glasgow. On my routes was Berriedale Avenue in Cathcart. And I have been down Berriedale Avenue in the morning on my bicycle and seen Professor Barclay sitting in his bay window reading. Even in those days I knew that this man was a remarkable scholar. But I only learned to appreciate his scholarship much later in life. But it is utterly amazing how such a remarkable scholar could arrive at the conclusions that he sometimes arrived at. I want to share his views for a moment because his mistaken views will teach us a valuable lesson.

Miracle	Prof Barclay's view
Feeding of 5000	Jesus embarrassed everyone into bringing their lunches out and sharing them. No real miracle except what he calls a miraculous transformation of people into sharing.[7]
Walking on water	Jesus walked round the shore and they were nearly at the shore when they saw him. And He comforted them by coming to them in their hour of struggle. No miracle here except in terms of his miraculous caring for people.[8]

And yet with reference to the feeding of the 5000 we note that:

[11] Jesus then took the loaves, and when he had given thanks, he distributed them to those who were seated; so also the fish, as much as they wanted. [12] And when they had eaten

---

[7] The Daily Study Bible: The Gospel of John Vol 1, p206 by William Barclay.
[8] The Daily Study Bible: The Gospel of John Vol 1, p212 by William Barclay.

their fill, he told his disciples, "Gather up the fragments left over, that nothing may be lost." [13] So they gathered them up and filled twelve baskets with fragments from the five barley loaves, left by those who had eaten. [14] When the people saw the sign which he had done, they said, "This is indeed the prophet who is to come into the world!"

- It specifically says that He took the loaves the boy had given Him.

- It says He took the fish the boy had given Him.

- And note v13, it says all the fragments left over came from the original five loaves and two fishes.

- And it specifically says that when the people saw this sign they believed that He was the prophet who was to come into the world. What sign? The sign that He could make them embarrassed? Clearly not.

When it came to the walking on water. Professor Barclay fails to take into consideration Matthew's account of this event in which not only does Jesus walk on water but so does Peter. He fails to take into account the statement of Matthew when he says

[24] but by this time the boat, battered by the waves, was far from the land, for the wind was against them.

They weren't by the shore and Jesus standing in safety on the shore calling out to them. He was walking amidst the waves and they thought it a ghost but Jesus identified Himself. He walked towards them and helped Peter to walk on water before helping Peter to get back into the boat and He entered Himself.

Professor Barclay was a very smart man, but he has come up with some crazy suggestions and has been confounded by his own cleverness. What is the problem here? And why am I bringing it up? I am not bringing it up in order to insult the memory of Professor Barclay. I will continue to use his writings and find them helpful in most cases. But the point of the matter is this… Professor Barclay's Jesus is too small!!!

He couldn't conceive of Jesus just simply feeding 12000 people with a small boy's lunch. But why not! He couldn't conceive of Jesus walking across the storm tossed sea, calming the storm at a word, and transporting that boat immediately to its destination. But why not? It is a simple truth that His Jesus is too small. Ours must not be!

Conclusion:

How big is your Jesus today? Is He a limited Jesus that can only do certain things, or is He Son of God as suggested and proved by John's Gospel. Are there limits to how much we will trust Him because if the truth be told we are more like Prof Barclay than we care to think? Are we small and struggling and sure to fail? Or are we allies of the King of Kings and Lord of Lords, the Son of God and Creator of the Universe and everything in it? In our hearts is He the King who spoke the worlds into existence and can do everything and anything and hence the victory is ours no matter what!

Which Jesus do you think He would have you believe in? And when we make our plans to reach out and preach the gospel in our community, or our city, or our land He would have you believe that the victory is ours already because of who our King is. Jesus is saying to us, "Believe me if you need me to walk on water, I can"!

Discussion Points:

1. What benefit can you see in dealing with a Jesus who can calm the storm?

2. What lesson do you think there is in the experience of Peter in this incident?

3. What kind of experiences in life frightens you?

4. In what way do you see Jesus addressing those fears?

5. Why do you think Jesus withdrew to the mountain alone? Is there a lesson in this for us?

6. What would it have felt like to have been with those disciples in a small boat in a violent storm on the Sea of Galilee?

7. If you had been in the boat, what would have gone through your mind when you saw Jesus walking on the water towards you?

8. Would you have been prepared to do what Peter did?

9. What does this passage teach us about the faith of Peter?

10. Is your faith greater or smaller than Peter's?

11. Why do you think Jesus walked on the water? Could He not have just transported Himself to the other side?

Chapter Ten

The Sixth Sign: A Man Born Blind

W E NOTICE FROM THE TITLE of this chapter that it is not just the healing of a blind man, but of a man who was born blind. And this is significant. The first few verses of John chapter nine linger on this point and a fallacy which had formed part of Jewish thinking was exposed and dealt with by the Master. And this is interesting to us because it is still a fallacy that is believed today. This man, who was born blind, was healed by Jesus.

Read John 9:1-41.

Who Sinned?

The chapter begins with this intriguing question, "Who sinned? That this man should be born blind, who sinned?" The Jews unhesitatingly connected suffering and sin. There was an assumption made by those disciples that if someone was suffering some kind of illness, or affliction of any kind then it must be the result of a punishment from God for sin. Who is responsible for the sin, ask the disciples that this man should be born blind?

When the friends of Job came to see him when he was in such suffering and pain, their first assumption was that he must have done something sinful and if only he would repent and turn away from sin then surely God would remove his suffering from him.

*7 "Think now, who that was innocent ever perished?
Or where were the upright cut off? 8 As I have seen, those
who plow iniquity and sow trouble reap the same. 9 By the
breath of God they perish, and by the blast of his anger they
are consumed. Job 4:7-9*

Today we call someone a Job's comforter if they offer no real comfort at all. Here in the story of Job they come to the great man of God who is in the midst of great suffering and they offer him an explanation. You must have done something very bad to be punished this way. Turn away from the evil in your life and you will be spared any more suffering.

The trouble in this case was that this man met by Jesus had been born blind? Who sinned that he should suffer so? Was it him? Or his parents?

And as we think about the question we wonder, how could it possibly be due to his own sin, if he had been born blind? Had he sinned before his birth? To that question, Jewish theologians gave an answer. They actually believed that a man could begin to sin while he was still in his mother's womb. They believed that evil began to have sway on a person from the moment of conception not from the moment of birth. And hence they would say, you could sin in the womb.

Presumably, mothers must ask themselves the question that if your unborn baby sinned, would you be aware of it? Would that explain so much heartburn and other problems? Clearly the idea is ludicrous and Jesus does not give a moment's consideration to such a way-out theory. Jesus gives no credence to prenatal sin.

But is it a punishment for his parents' sin? There can be little doubt that children often do suffer because of parents' sin. If a parent were a drunkard or an abuser then the child would suffer as a result. But it should be noted that the guilt of sin is not something that can or will be passed on by God. We see this in a number of passages. And it satisfies our need for natural justice to know that God will not hold us accountable for anyone's sin but our own. I will not be lost because of my father's sin or my grandfather's, or great great... great great grandfather's nor Adam's sin. I may be lost because of my own sin but no one else's. We revisit a passage in Ezekiel.

> *[20] The soul that sins shall die. The son shall not suffer for the iniquity of the father, nor the father suffer for the iniquity of the son; the righteousness of the righteous shall be upon himself, and the wickedness of the wicked shall be upon himself. Ezek 18:20*

God will not impute guilt to us because of Adam's sin or our father's sin or anyone else's sin but our own.

Some point to Exodus 20 in this connection which says that God visits the sins of the fathers upon the children to the third and fourth generation. This was a reference to Israel who were taken into captivity because of the idolatry and disobedience of the nation. They spent 70 years in captivity so that it was a new generation who returned to possess the land. There were children who were born in Babylon who were not guilty of idolatry but they suffered captivity because of their forefather's sin. They suffered the consequences of their parents' sin but not the guilt of it.

So what is the real answer? Jesus is somewhat enigmatic about His reply. But the answer is there for all to see.

> *"It was not that this man sinned, or his parents, but that the works of God might be made manifest in him. [4] We must work the works of him who sent me, while it is day; night comes, when no one can work. [5] As long as I am in the world, I am the light of the world."*

Jesus says that it was nothing to do with his sin, prenatal or postnatal. It was nothing to do with his parents' sin at all. But that the works of God might be made manifest we must take opportunity to work the works of God whilst there is opportunity to do so.

In his contemporary commentary/translation called The Message, Eugene H. Peterson, renders this section in the following way…

> *Jesus said, "You're asking the wrong question. You're looking for someone to blame. There is no such cause-effect here. Look instead for what God can do.*

Peterson has captured the heart of the passage. It is not about blame, it is about opportunity. Never mind who is to blame, but now that the opportunity is given, the glory of God will be seen.

There is a tendency for man to think that whenever any calamity comes upon him that it must be a punishment. A child is born with a disability... whose fault is it? And this is not a helpful or healthy response. Jesus would hear nothing of it in John chapter nine. It is not about fault or blame... it is about God using opportunity to bring blessing and demonstrate His glory. Jesus is going to use this opportunity to demonstrate His grace and loving kindness.

Sabbath Matters!

Now again we see that Jesus gets himself into hot water over the Jewish regulations for the Sabbath. We take pains to point out that He is in hot water over the regulations that man has added onto God's law concerning the Sabbath.

Jesus fell foul of the man made Sabbath regulations in more than one way:

1. By making clay of his spittle:

To do the simplest acts on the Sabbath day was to be guilty of working on the Sabbath. By making the clay to anoint the man's eyes they would have viewed this as working on the Sabbath. In fact there were a multitude of such regulations:

- A man may not fill a dish with oil and put it beside a lamp and put the end of the wick in it.

- A man may not extinguish a candle on the Sabbath.

- A man may not go out on the Sabbath with sandals shod with nails (the weight of the nails would have constituted a burden and to carry a burden was to break the Sabbath.)

- A man may not cut his fingernails or pull a hair out of his head or beard.

Believe it or not it was specifically forbidden to heal on the Sabbath. Medical attention could only be given if life was in actual danger, and even then it must be such as to keep the patient from getting worse, but it must not make him any better. e.g. If a man's hand were dislocated, he may not pour cold water over it. It was forbidden to set a broken limb.

Clearly the man who was born blind was in no danger of his life, therefore in their view, Jesus broke the Sabbath when he healed him. Jesus has a one-word answer to all of this… Baloney!

In their drive to cover every eventuality and all minutiae, they had lost sight of what God's law was all about. God's law for the Sabbath was not concerned with whether or not a man had nails in his sandals. It was concerned with whether or not a man had God in his heart. Whether he was setting time aside for God and being God's man.

The Journey of Faith.

Then finally we come to the journey of faith in this passage which is undertaken by the man. In some ways we could say that every man is on the journey of faith and it is a question of what stage they have reached in their journey of faith.

Who is the Jesus who did this remarkable sign?

> [26] They said to him, "What did he do to you? How did he open your eyes?" [27] He answered them, "I have told you already, and you would not listen. Why do you want to hear it again? Do you too want to become his disciples?" [28] And they reviled him, saying, "You are his disciple, but we are disciples of Moses. [29] We know that God has spoken to Moses, but as for this man, we do not know where he comes from." [30] The man answered, "Why, this is a marvel! You do not know where he comes from, and yet he opened my eyes. [31] We know that God does not listen to sinners, but if any one is a worshiper of God and does his will, God listens to him. [32] Never since the world began has it been heard that any one opened the eyes of a man born blind. [33] If this man were not

from God, he could do nothing."[34] *They answered him, "You were born in utter sin, and would you teach us?" And they cast him out.*

The argument of the Pharisees was plain enough to understand:-

1. Jesus had broken the Sabbath and was a sinner.
2. The blind man was under punishment for sin and could not instruct them.
3. Hence the blind man should be cast out of the synagogue for being a disciple of the sinner Jesus who would lead the people away from God.

But the argument of the blind man was simple and devastating to their case.

1. I am no theologian or trained scholar but this much I know, God does not listen to sinners.
2. Because of the sign that this man has done, it is clear that God listens to this man.
3. No one since the foundation of the world has brought sight to a man born blind. But this man has. Hence he is a prophet of God.

This argument was so devastating to their case that they were enraged at him and decided to cast him out of the synagogue.

We must note the journey of faith that the man makes in John 9. For it is the same journey of faith made by all men today. All of us are somewhere on that same journey and we must identify where we are. Note the stages of the journey as we see them in John 9. We see the stages clearly in the ways in which the blind man refers to Jesus at different points in the story.

a. *"The man called Jesus made clay and anointed my eyes."(v11)*

b. *"What do you say about him, since he has opened your eyes?"*
He said, "He is a prophet." (v17)

c. [35] *Jesus heard that they had cast him out, and having found*
him he said, "Do you believe in the Son of Man?" [36] *He*
answered, "And who is he, sir, that I may believe in him?"

[37] *Jesus said to him, "You have seen him, and it is he who*
speaks to you." [38] *He said, "Lord, I believe"; and he worshiped*
him.

Conclusion:

Do we see the path of progress through the chapter?

The man Jesus:

At one stage in our journey Jesus is just a man. He is a man who
says and does remarkable things that we have never bothered too
much to learn about because that is all that he is, a man. And to many
inhabitants of our city and our homeland, Jesus is just a man. The
blind man had come along and met the man Jesus, who made clay
out of spittle and anointed his eyes. There are a number of people
you know today who are like this; they only know Jesus as some man
who lived a long time ago. We need to challenge them out of this cul-
de-sac. We need to challenge them to read the gospels with us. My
approach to studying with people is to take them to the gospels and
we read them together until we hope that they come away believing
that Jesus was more than just a man.

He is a Prophet:

The next stage in the development of the faith of the blind man
is when he came back seeing from Siloam. Siloam means sent because
the water was sent through a channel carved out of the solid rock
under the instructions of King Hezekiah to protect Jerusalem from
siege. But the name of the pool took on a whole new meaning when
Jesus sent the blind man to the pool and he came back seeing. No man
can do the things which Jesus did unless he was a prophet sent from

God. If He is a prophet then we need to listen to Him. Hence we need to turn to the book and listen to Jesus. Turn to the book of Acts to see how to become a Christian. Turn to the Sermon on the Mount and the epistles to see how we ought to live as a Christian. If He is the prophet then people today need to listen to Him too.

Son of God:

The purpose in John's writing is to bring us to the point where we see Jesus as the Son of God. The incident with the blind man is just one sign of many which brings us to faith in Him. We see the difference in the blind man when he reached the end of his journey of faith. *"I believe… and he worshipped Him!"*

Every man is somewhere on that journey. We want to help everyone to reach the end of the journey whereby they see Jesus as He should be seen, as Son of God. Since every man is somewhere on that journey, it is good if we understand the journey and can see where we are ourselves. And when we consider the purpose of this book, to encourage and help us to be sharing the gospel message with a lost world, we are moved to think about others surrounding us. Who do you know who needs help along the journey? We want to help them, our friends, neighbors, family, enemies. Ask them if they would read the New Testament with us. If they don't have one, we'll give them one. Ask this week and help them along the journey of faith.

Discussion Points:

1. What important lesson did Jesus have for us in our way of looking at disability and sickness?

2. Why do you think Jesus did not just instantly heal the man, without the need to make clay or send the man to the pool?

3. In what ways did Jesus "break the Sabbath"?

4. Did Jesus disobey the Law given by God to Moses?

5. If Jesus could heal a man born blind, what might He be able to do for us?

6. Before you began reading the New Testament, where would you have seen yourself on the journey of faith described in this chapter?

7. Where are you now on the journey of faith?

Chapter Eleven

The Seventh Sign: Dead Man Walking

IN OUR SPECIAL SERIES ON the seven signs in John's Gospel we come in this chapter to the seventh of the signs. We recall that the purpose of the recording of these signs is to produce faith.

> *30 Now Jesus did many other signs in the presence of the disciples, which are not written in this book; 31 but these are written that you may believe that Jesus is the Christ, the Son of God, and that believing you may have life in his name. Jn 20:30-31.*

As such it is profitable for those who are not yet sure about Jesus, and we will find that it is profitable for us when we lack faith or find doubts creeping into our lives, and faith floundering. We need to turn again and again to these accounts and build up our faith in Christ, by reading them over and over again.

In turn we have looked at each of the signs and thought about what it means for us today, what it means about Jesus and how He is able to help. From the water turned to wine in Cana, to the healing of the nobleman's son at a distance, through the healing of the lame man at the pool of Bethzatha, through the feeding of the 5000 by Bethsaida Julias, through the walking on the water, and then last time through the healing of the man born blind, we have seen marvelous things about our Master Jesus.

Now we turn to the last of these seven signs: The Raising of Lazarus. The story is contained in ch 11. Read John 11:1-53.

This was not the first time that Jesus had dealt with death, and dealt with it successfully. In fact, in the gospel records we find Jesus raising the dead on three occasions. To have dealt with death once would be often enough and ultimate proof beyond proof. But to have dealt with it three times says, Believe in Me… Believe in Me,… Believe in Me!!

Matt 9:18-26.	Raising of the daughter of Jairus: A young girl of 12 years of age had died. Jesus arrived just too late to heal her, and on taking his inner group of three disciples into the house with Him, He gently took her hand and raised her up. She sat up and took food and was restored to her family once more.
Luke 7:11-16.	Jesus was entering the city of Nain when He was met by a funeral procession on the way out of Nain. A young man was to be buried and his mother was distraught following the body as it was carried out of the town. She was a widow and now even her son had been taken. Jesus was moved with compassion at the sight and stops the funeral procession to lay hands on the boy and bring him back to life.

In both cases Jesus was moved with great compassion for the grieving relatives. In both cases a young person had died, and in both cases the healing was instantaneous.

Lazarus the Special Case.

Lazarus is mentioned only in John's gospel and not at all in Matthew, Mark or Luke. However his sisters, Mary and Martha are mentioned in

Luke 10:38-42 where we are told that Jesus is a guest in their home. It is clear that they have a home in which Jesus felt welcome and this may well have been a lodging place for Jesus on his regular visits to Jerusalem throughout His public ministry. Bethany was only two miles from Jerusalem and would have been an ideal place to stay.

We can be sure then that Jesus knew these people well. Mary and Martha catered for his needs and Lazarus would have been well known to Jesus as a friend.

> *⁵ Now Jesus loved Martha and her sister and Lazarus.*

Barclay and others make much of the omission of the story of the raising of Lazarus from the other gospel accounts. However it should be realized that no one gospel account is exhaustive. John records the raising of Lazarus but says nothing about the widow's son nor Jairus. Yet it is Luke alone who mentions the raising at Nain. John not only mentions the raising of Lazarus but also explains to us the strategic importance of this particular miracle.

Two things should be noted about this miracle which make it important.

1. Death and Delay.

One of the strangest aspects of this miracle is contained in v6. Especially is this strange after what is said in v5.

> *⁵ Now Jesus loved Martha and her sister and Lazarus. ⁶ So when he heard that he was ill, he stayed two days longer in the place where he was.*

Now this is a strange statement to make. We might have expected it to say that Jesus loved Mary and Martha and Lazarus so He made all haste to get to Bethany as soon as He possibly could, wasting no time whatsoever in making sure He got there before anything disastrous might happen to His close friend in Bethany.

But instead of that it says that He loved these three close friends, one of whom was desperately ill so He delayed His journey by two whole days. Note however the chronology of this miracle.

Day 1	Mary and Martha desperately worried send word to Jesus	Lazarus dies on the very day Jesus is informed
Day 2	Jesus delays departure	2nd day Lazarus is dead
Day 3	Jesus delays departure	3rd day Lazarus is dead
Day 4	Jesus comes to raise a corpse	4th day Lazarus is dead and the day of his resurrection.

Given this information it becomes clear that Lazarus must have died on the very day that word was sent. When we see this it becomes clear that there was no reason at all to hurry and perhaps some good reasons to delay. Notice how Jesus refers to this later in v14-15:

> *[14] Then Jesus told them plainly, "Lazarus is dead; [15] and for your sake I am glad that I was not there, so that you may believe. But let us go to him."*

In each of the other cases of raising the dead, the young people had only just died. In fact at that time and in that climate, people were buried without delay, on the same day as their death. They had no refrigeration to keep bodies for any longer and so burial took place immediately.

Some might have hypothesized that perhaps these young people were not actually dead. Perhaps they were in a particularly deep coma. This is not possible with Lazarus. Lazarus had been dead four days in the tomb. There is no possibility that he is still alive. And indeed, all there knew it. Martha is the down to earth practical one of the family and she says it very plainly.

> *[39] Jesus said, "Take away the stone." Martha, the sister of the dead man, said to him, "Lord, by this time there will be an odor, for he has been dead four days."*

By the time Jesus heard the news, Lazarus was already dead and haste would add nothing to the situation. Jesus deliberately waited two more days in order that Mary and Martha might not only be brought joy at the restoration of their brother but might be brought even more joy at the understanding and faith they will be brought to by the Resurrection and the Life, Jesus. Jesus waited two more days to come and raise a stinking corpse.

A dead man, indisputably dead, walked out of the tomb in order that all men might know that He is Lord of Life, He is the Resurrection and the Life.

2. Dead Man's Testimony.

Jesus's own testimony concerning what He was about to do is contained in v40.

> *40 Jesus said to her, "Did I not tell you that if you would believe you would see the glory of God?"*

For this reason He had come! For this reason He had delayed His coming! For this reason He offered up ultimate proof of His I AM claim to Martha and Mary.

This is what it is all about. It was necessary that they should see the glory of God and the glory of God's Messiah. Messiah has come and all must know. And in order that they might know without a shadow of doubt, dead Lazarus must walk unaided from the tomb.

John tells this story because of its strategic importance in the story of Jesus. There is now only a few short days until the crucifixion of Jesus. When the Jews saw what Jesus had done in raising Lazarus, they strengthened their resolve to do away with the Master.

We can't let this go on! If we do then we shall be completely sidelined. Everyone will turn and believe in Him and we shall be left with nothing. The Romans will discard us and deal directly with this Jesus and hence the plot which had been brewing for three years was now firmed up in the secret meetings being held in Jerusalem.

> *53 So from that day on they took counsel how to put him to death.*

Because of who He is and how the people loved Him, because of His revolutionary teaching, because of the way He discarded the oral traditions of the elders, because of the many signs that He has done drawing the attention of all Israel towards Him, and now because of the raising of Lazarus— Jesus had to go.

The time has come and Jesus must be disposed of before there is nothing at all left. This miracle, occurring as it did only two miles from Jerusalem, and occurring when it did just a few days before the Passover, was strategically very important in raising the profile of Jesus before the nation and stimulating the open hostility and opposition of those who were more concerned with their prominence and position than they were with the will of God. The difference between Jesus and these Jewish bureaucrats was stark.

1. They were prepared to sacrifice the nation in order to preserve their own importance and position.

2. Jesus was prepared to sacrifice himself in order to preserve for himself a spiritual nation.

Therein lies the difference. As we go into chapter 12 we see how this developed.

> *¹ Six days before the Passover, Jesus came to Bethany, where Lazarus was, whom Jesus had raised from the dead. ² There they made him a supper; Martha served, and Lazarus was one of those at table with him. ³ Mary took a pound of costly ointment of pure nard and anointed the feet of Jesus and wiped his feet with her hair; and the house was filled with the fragrance of the ointment. ⁴ But Judas Iscariot, one of his disciples (he who was to betray him), said, ⁵ "Why was this ointment not sold for three hundred denarii and given to the poor?" ⁶ This he said, not that he cared for the poor but because he was a thief, and as he had the money box he used to take what was put into it. ⁷ Jesus said, "Let her alone, let her keep it for the day of my burial. ⁸ The poor you always have with you, but you do not always have me." ⁹ When the*

> *great crowd of the Jews learned that he was there, they came, not only on account of Jesus but also to see Lazarus, whom he had raised from the dead. [10] So the chief priests planned to put Lazarus also to death, [11] because on account of him many of the Jews were going away and believing in Jesus. Jn 12:1-11.*

The event is a celebration dinner in Bethany just outside Jerusalem and many no doubt came to witness a dead man walk and talk and eat. There can be little doubt of the impact of this event on Jerusalem. They came, they saw and they went away believing.

This led in the very next verse to the Palm Sunday triumphal entry, and the Palm Sunday Triumphal entry led to the crucifixion of our Lord.

Everyone understood the importance of this event. Dead men don't rise! Lazarus rose and Jesus established beyond all doubt that He is the Messiah of God.

I Am the Resurrection and the Life:

Before we close this chapter we have to look at the important statement that Jesus was trying to establish in our minds by this miracle which He performed.

One of the remarkable things about this chapter which is often overlooked is Martha's statement of faith.

Given that Martha is supposed to be the less spiritual of the two sisters, the one more concerned about serving tables and practical matters like how a corpse would smell if the stone were rolled away, her confession of faith is doubly remarkable. Let us look at what Martha said when prompted by Jesus to make her great confession.

> [20] *When Martha heard that Jesus was coming, she went and met him, while Mary sat in the house. [21] Martha said to Jesus, "Lord, if you had been here, my brother would not have died. [22] And even now I know that whatever you ask from God, God will give you." [23] Jesus said to her, "Your brother will rise again." [24] Martha said to him, "I know*

that he will rise again in the resurrection at the last day."
25 Jesus said to her, "I am the resurrection and the life; he
who believes in me, though he die, yet shall he live, 26 and
whoever lives and believes in me shall never die. Do you
believe this?" 27 She said to him, "Yes, Lord; I believe that
you are the Christ, the Son of God, he who is coming into
the world."

Martha declares herself to be a great woman of faith:

1. Lord if you had been here my brother would not have died.
2. Even now that He is dead you can still do something
3. I believe in the resurrection at the last day
4. I believe that you are the Christ
5. I believe that you are the Son of God
6. I believe that you are the one who is coming into the world!

There is no more comprehensive statement of faith in all the Scripture than this! And it is the statement of faith that we all must come to in our lives also! Oh that we all, and all whom we know and love could come to the same statement of faith as this!

Conclusion:

You have to reach the point that you can say with Martha this confession of faith. You have to accept the teaching of Jesus to Martha that day— that as far as you are concerned Jesus is the Resurrection and the Life.

In the same way that He called forth Lazarus from the tomb so also shall He one day call you. Do you believe this?

If you live and believe in Jesus, you will never truly die… perhaps physically stop breathing but in every way that is important and eternally significant, you will never die. Do you believe this? Echo with Martha the words of her great confession today. Can you echo the words of Martha today?

"Yes, Lord; I believe that you are the Christ, the Son of God, he who is coming into the world."

Discussion Points:

1. What would you consider to be the most dramatic sign that Jesus could have performed?

2. Why was the delay of four days a crucial element of this sign?

3. Can you describe the impact this sign may have had on the family of Lazarus?

4. What kind of impact do you think it would have had on the small village of Bethany?

5. In what way did this miracle have a deciding influence on the religious leaders of the Jews?

6. What kind of faith did Martha have?

7. What kind of faith do you have?

8. Are you ready to make the kind of confession of faith that Martha did?

9. What other kind of evidence could there be that would be greater than this?

Chapter Twelve
The Ultimate Sign: The Sign of Jonah

IN OUR STUDY OF JOHN'S gospel we are now nearing a conclusion. We have looked at the seven signs that John presented, evidence that Jesus is the Son of God. That was his purpose all along. He wrote the book in order that you might believe. And now he has presented evidence after evidence that you might come to believe in this Jesus. In the very opening words of his book he stated his purpose. It was in order that we might see that in the beginning was the Word and the Word was with God and *the Word was God… and the Word became flesh and dwelt among us full of grace and truth; we have beheld his glory, glory as of the only Son from the Father.*

His goal was to present the Word of God that we might believe in Him… and each sign in turn focused our attention on Him. And the….

1. Water was turned into wine in Cana of Galilee…

2. The official's son was healed at a distance…

3. The lame man was healed at the pool of Bethzatha in Jerusalem…

4. The great multitude were fed by a few scraps of food…

5. Jesus came walking on the water and stilled the storm…

6. The man born blind was given sight by being sent to the pool called "Sent"...

7. And dead Lazarus walked out of the grave to show that the Word has power over life and death and calls dead men back to life.

Only one sign remains and it is the most crucial sign of all. This is the ultimate, the crux of the matter. Is the bodily resurrection of Christ a true event of history or is it the false base for a false religion? Both friends and enemies of the Christian faith have recognized the resurrection of Christ to be the foundation stone of the faith.

Paul in writing to the Corinthians said this:

"... if Christ has not been raised, then our preaching is in vain and your faith is in vain." (1 Corinthians 15:14.)

Either the resurrection is the greatest event in human history in which man finds his ultimate salvation... or it is the greatest and cruelest of illusions, which has duped many to go to a meaningless death. If He did rise, it was the most sensational event in all history, and we have conclusive answers to the profound questions of our existence. Where have we come from? Why are we here? Where are we going?

If Christ arose, we know with certainty that God exists, what He is like, and how we may know Him personally. We have to make a major revision to our worldview and take into account all that Jesus taught us. The universe takes on meaning and purpose, and it is possible to experience the living God in contemporary Dundee, Glasgow, Leeds or Delhi.

However, if He did not rise from the dead then Christianity is an interesting anachronism, a strange museum piece, nothing more. It has no objective validity or reality. The martyrs who went singing to the lions, and even in the last century, those missionaries who gave their lives willingly were nothing more than poor deluded fools.

Hence the doctrine of the resurrection of the Christ is either the greatest good for mankind or one of the greatest evils. It cannot be anything in between.

We should note that the concept of the resurrection did not develop accidentally. Neither was it an idle tale invented by the disciples. For Jesus repeatedly made reference to his death and resurrection during the three and a half years of his public ministry.

> *¹⁹ Jesus answered them, "Destroy this temple, and in three days I will raise it up." ²⁰ The Jews then said, "It has taken forty-six years to build this temple, and will you raise it up in three days?" ²¹ But he spoke of the temple of his body.*
> *John 2:19-21*

> *⁴⁰ For as Jonah was three days and three nights in the belly of the whale, so will the Son of man be three days and three nights in the heart of the earth.   Matthew 12:40*

> *³⁰ They went on from there and passed through Galilee. And he would not have any one know it; ³¹ for he was teaching his disciples, saying to them, "The Son of man will be delivered into the hands of men, and they will kill him; and when he is killed, after three days he will rise."   Mark 9:30-31*

We note that Jesus staked His whole credibility on the idea that He would rise again. If He was not raised, then we should not listen to Him ... He was a charlatan and a fraud. But if He was indeed raised.... if after three days that tomb was indeed empty, then it validates everything He ever said and taught us, and we should listen to Him with full attention, for He has the words of life and is indeed our hope and our salvation.

Take time to read John chapters 19, 20 and 21. If you are in a home Bible study now, share the reading with others in the room. Read it prayerfully and carefully, considering the experience of Jesus as He gave His life as a ransom for all. This is a poignant and powerful account. This is what Jesus said would be that which would draw all men to Him.

In the thirties, a remarkable attack on the resurrection was launched by a young British lawyer. He was convinced that the resurrection was a mere tissue of fable and fantasy. Sensing that it was the foundation stone of the Christian faith, he decided to do the world a favor by once and for all exposing this fraud and superstition. As a lawyer, he felt he had the critical faculties to sift the evidence and to admit nothing as evidence which did not meet the stiff criteria for admission into a law court.

However, while he was doing his research a remarkable thing happened. The case was not nearly as easy as he had supposed. As a result, the first chapter of his book is entitled, "The Book That Refused to Be Written." In it he describes how as he examined the evidence, he became persuaded against his will, of the fact of the bodily resurrection. The book is called "Who Moved the Stone?" and the author is Frank Morrison. It has become a classic defense of the resurrection of Jesus.

There are in fact two vital parts to the evidence concerning the resurrection of Christ.

1. The Empty Tomb
2. The Resurrection Appearances.

Both of these pieces of evidence require to be examined before we close our mind to the case. The court is now assembled, the witnesses are gathered, we are the jury, let us hear the case and decide the verdict, and make the most important judgment of our lives.

1. The Empty Tomb.

Other religions have shrines where their leaders were buried, but Christianity stands unique amongst the religions of the world for what it has is an empty tomb. This fact has to be reckoned with and since the events of that fateful weekend in Jerusalem, friends and foes of Christianity have been making their arguments about the empty tomb. How can we account for the empty tomb?

There have been only a few reasoned suggestions made to account for the empty tomb and we shall examine these briefly:

a. Disciples stole the body.

This was the earliest explanation that was circulated. It was the reaction of the chief priests and the elders when the guards gave them the infuriating and mysterious news that the body was gone.

> *[11] While they were going, behold, some of the guard went into the city and told the chief priests all that had taken place. [12] And when they had assembled with the elders and taken counsel, they gave a sum of money to the soldiers [13] and said, "Tell people, 'His disciples came by night and stole him away while we were asleep.' [14] And if this comes to the governor's ears, we will satisfy him and keep you out of trouble." [15] So they took the money and did as they were directed; and this story has been spread among the Jews to this day. Matthew 28:11-15*

They gave the soldiers money and told them to explain that the disciples had come at night and stolen the body whilst they were asleep. That story is such an obvious fabrication that Matthew does not even bother to refute it. What judge would listen to you if you said that whilst you were asleep your neighbor came into your house and stole your television set? How would you know what had happened if you were asleep at the time? Testimony like this would be laughed out of court.

There were two further things wrong with this theory. First of all, it was foreign to the ethical standards and behavior of the disciples. Further, it would mean that they were perpetrators of a deliberate lie, which was responsible for the ultimate deaths of thousands of people. That is not the character of the disciples of Jesus. Secondly, it should be remembered that these disciples gave their lives for their testimony concerning the empty tomb. It is one thing to tell a lie to deceive others, but to go to death yourself for something you know to be a lie is beyond belief. If the disciples had actually stolen the body, surely they would have told the truth on the point of death and rescued themselves.

b. Authorities stole the body.

The second hypothesis was that the authorities, either Jewish or Roman stole the body. But why? Having put guards at the tomb, what would have been their reason for removing the body? And what is even more damning to this theory is, why after the disciples began to declare the resurrection message, why did they remain silent? Why did they not immediately speak up and declare it all to be a trick, and produce the body, dragging it through the streets of Jerusalem so that everyone could see and give no credence to the declaration of resurrection appearances. That would have been a very simple solution to all their problems. They could have strangled Christianity in its cradle, and it would never have grown to be believed throughout the world as it is today. But they could not do it. They did not have the body to produce. They were mystified as to what they could do. They arrested the apostles (Acts 4) and they threatened them, instructing them to desist from telling the resurrection message. But no matter how hard they tried, they could not silence it. They could not silence the eloquent testimony of an empty tomb. Their guards and seals had been set in an attempt to stop the tomb being empty. But no guards or seals could withstand the Christ's resurrection.

c. The Wrong Tomb.

A third theory propounded was that the women went to the wrong tomb. Those women were distraught and overcome with grief, and in the early morning gloom, they simply went to the wrong tomb. In their distress, they imagined that Jesus had risen because they found an empty tomb.

However, this theory is very easily destroyed. If the women went to the wrong tomb, why did not the disciples go to the right tomb? And even more important, why did not the Jews and Romans simply point out the mistake as soon as the preaching of resurrection occurred. Certainly Joseph of Arimathea, the owner of the tomb could have settled the matter once and for all. Further it should be remembered that this was not some large uniform public cemetery with a thousand graves all the same. There was no other tomb there that would have allowed them to make a mistake.

d. The Swoon Theory.

The swoon theory was a fourth hypothesis which has been put forward. In this view, Christ did not actually die. He was mistakenly reported as dead, but He had in fact fainted, and (they say) in the coolness of the tomb He revived and came out of the tomb, appearing to the disciples who mistakenly reported Him as risen from the dead. This is a theory of modern construction. It first appeared at the end of the 18th century. Not one suggestion has come down from antiquity of this nature. But for the sake of argument, let us assume that they are right. Jesus did not actually die, but swooned.

He survived three days in the tomb without....

- medical attention despite His horrific wounds
- water
- food or any other sustenance to revive Him

And it should be remembered that He survived swathed in burial clothes which were covered in burial spices. Could He have survived in such circumstances?

- Where did He get the strength to get out of the burial clothes?
- Where did He get the strength to push the huge stone away from the front of the tomb?
- How did He get past the guards that had been placed there?
- And once He had done that how did He then walk miles on feet that had been pierced with spikes to get away from the district?

Even some of Christianity's fiercest critics have been scathing about the viability of this theory. David Strauss, the German critic, who does not believe in the resurrection, rejected the idea as incredible. He said, *"It is impossible that one who had just come forth from the grave, half dead, who crept about weak and ill, who stood in the need of medical treatment, of bandaging, strengthening, and tender care, and who at last succumbed to suffering, could ever have given the disciples the impression that He was a conqueror over death and the grave; that He was the Prince of Life".* Finally of course, if this theory is correct, Christ Himself was involved in flagrant lies. His disciples believed He had been dead and come back to life, Jesus did nothing to dispel this thought, indeed He commended those who accepted this and encouraged them to go throughout the world preaching it.

When each of the theories is examined in turn, we find nothing to commend them. When rather we see that reliable witnesses testified that the dead Christ rose, that the tomb was empty on that Sunday morning. They suffered death rather than change their testimony by one sentence, one word, or one comma. We have the kind of evidence that would be acceptable in any court of law in any country in any age. The empty tomb proclaims the risen Christ, then and now, and its evidence is incontrovertible.

Another important consideration is that the claim that Jesus had risen from the dead was first published in the very city where it was reported to have happened and no one was able to disprove it or contradict it. Suppose the resurrection was alleged to have happened in Glasgow, Scotland and was first declared and preached in Delhi, India! We might say that we would only have the words of those people in Delhi who proclaimed it. How could they know? How do we know that these things are so because Glasgow is a long way away. We can't go to the tomb; we can't talk to the witnesses.

We see that He rose in Jerusalem and the preaching began there amongst the witnesses and all could go to the garden tomb and assure themselves it was indeed empty. Clearly the people who were closest to the event in history and who would most assuredly have wanted to put a stop to such a report were powerless in the face of the facts at hand. The apostles preached a resurrected Christ in a place and at a time when it was fully possible to check every piece of evidence, to interrogate every witness and to expose any trace of fraud.

The only reasonable conclusion is that they were telling the truth and had nothing to fear from an investigation of their claim. Many of the apostles spent their whole lives preaching the resurrected Christ under the most difficult and trying of circumstances. They were cursed, hated, driven out of cities, imprisoned and tortured because of their message. Many died as martyrs. Would this group of men have been so motivated by a story which they knew to be a lie? You know that is absurd.

2. The Resurrection Appearances

During the forty day period between His resurrection and ascension, there were ten recorded appearances that the Lord made to various individuals under different circumstances:

i.   Appeared to 3 women who came to the tomb. (Matthew 28:10)

ii.   Appeared to Mary Magdalene. (John 20:11-18)

iii.   Appeared to Simon Peter. (Luke 24:34)

iv.   Appeared to 2 disciples on road to Emmaus. (Luke 24:13-35)

v.   Appeared to 10 disciples in locked room with Thomas absent. (John 20:19-25)

vi.   Appeared to the 11 with Thomas present. (John 20:26-29)

vii.   Appeared to disciples as they were fishing. (John 21:1-23)

viii. Appeared to 500 brethren at one time. (1 Corinthians 15:6)

ix.   Appeared to James. (1 Corinthians 15:7)

x.   Appeared to all the disciples at the time of His ascension on the Mount of Olives. (Luke 24:50-52, Acts 1:3-10)

We see that there is a great diversity in the circumstances, timing and location of the appearances of Jesus. Some were in the garden near His tomb; some were in the upper room. One was on the road from Jerusalem to Emmaus, and some were far away in Galilee.

The major theory advanced to explain away the accounts of Christ is that they were hallucinations. At first this sounds like a plausible explanation of an otherwise supernatural event. Let us think about this explanation for a moment.

a. Hallucinations occur generally in people who tend to be vividly imaginative and of nervous disposition. But the appearances of Christ were to all sorts of people. True, some could be accused of being emotional women, but there were also hard-headed men like fishermen, a tax collector, and others of various dispositions.

b. Hallucinations are extremely subjective and individual. For this reason no two people have the same experience. But in the case of the resurrection, Christ appeared not just to individuals, but to groups, including one of more than 500 people.

c. Hallucinations usually occur only at particular times and places and are associated with the events fancied. But these appearances occurred both indoors and outdoors, in the morning, afternoon and evening.

If only Peter and James and John claimed to have seen Christ and none others, we might think that these three who had been so close to Jesus were so emotionally distraught over the events of their friend's death that they hallucinated. But there were hundreds of people involved as witnesses of the living Christ. They saw Him at different times and under different circumstances, but they were all positive in their identification.

d. Generally psychic experiences like this occur over a long period of time and with some regularity. But these experiences happened during a period of 40 days and then stopped abruptly. No one ever said they happened again. Who cured these people of their hallucinations?

e. Finally, we must note that in order to have an experience like this, one must so intensely want to believe that he projects something that really isn't there and attaches reality to his imagination. Suppose for instance a mother who has lost her son in the war remembers how he used to come home from work every evening at 6 o'clock. She sits in her rocking chair every afternoon musing and remembering. Finally she thinks she sees him come through the door at that time and has a conversation with him. At this point she has lost touch with reality.

But this was not the case with the disciples of Jesus. The women came with ointments to complete the burial. And when He appeared to them they did not believe it thinking that He was the gardener.

They were brought to belief against their expectation. When the other disciples heard, the Scripture says,

> *"... but these words seemed to them an idle tale, and they didn't believe them." (Luke 24:11.)*

Of course, the classic case is that of Thomas, who was not present on the first occasion when Jesus appeared to them in the locked room. They told him about it and he scoffed and said that unless he could feel the nail prints he would not believe. The story of what happened is told in John 20. Jesus appeared to him and invited him to touch and believe. Thomas fell down in worship and declared, *"My Lord and my God."*

To hold the hallucination theory in explaining the appearances of Christ, one must completely ignore the evidence.

Conclusion:

The most remarkable event of all history is declared by the empty tomb and the eyewitness testimony concerning a risen Christ. This is the bedrock of our faith. Here is the validation of everything that Jesus ever did and said. And we can place our faith in Him because of the empty tomb. He is Lord. He is risen. Believe in Him, trust Him, obey Him, follow Him.

> *Crown Him with many crowns.*
> *The Lamb upon His throne!*
> *Hark how the heavenly anthem drowns*
> *All music but its own!*
> *Awake my soul and sing*
> *Of Him who died for thee*
> *And hail Him as thy matchless King*
> *thro' all eternity.*
> *Matthew Bridges*

When fair and open minded people consider the crucifixion and resurrection of Christ, it has a profound and long lasting effect. They find themselves in this story. It becomes their story. His death becomes not some dry history but a living story that Christians for centuries have called the gospel, the good news of Jesus.

Discussion Points:

1. Why was the tomb of Jesus found to be empty?
2. Why is the empty tomb significant?
3. What has the empty tomb got to do with you?
4. How can we be certain that Jesus rose from the dead?
5. What are the implications if Jesus did not rise?
6. What are the implications if Jesus did rise?
7. What do we learn from the seven signs in John's gospel.
8. What do we learn from the resurrection of Christ?

The next step in this process of sharing the gospel would be to share the response to this fundamental truth from the book of Acts. In the Book of Acts in the New Testament, we see how people in the first century responded to the great news of the gospel of Christ. A study of the Book of Acts can make it clear how to become a Christian. In sharing the gospel with people in a home Bible study setting, I always make it clear that my earnest prayer for them is that they might become Christians in the same way that the Book of Acts indicates, the way thousands upon thousands did in the New Testament. I end by asking God to bless them in every way, that they might grow in the grace and the knowledge of our Lord Jesus Christ, and share with me in our pilgrimage to a heavenly home because of His great sacrifice.

Chapter Thirteen

I Believe Because... What is Man?

In SHARING THIS MANUSCRIPT WITH some colleagues and scholars, an interesting suggestion came back. There are times that some persistent questions remain in the mind of the seeker. I accept the message concerning Jesus but I am still wondering about this. The request that was made to me was to include some of the answers to basic questions that arise in the course of studying with people to lead them to Christ. And simply for peace of mind, some kind of answer should be given to some of these questions.

With that in mind, I am including some further information in the concluding chapters of this book.

In this work I have tried to present an approach to sharing the gospel simply by using the Word of God itself. It is my contention that the Word is still powerful to save, and that the Word of God is that which leads to the new birth. This thought is both Biblical and sure. This philosophy suggests that we must use the gospel records themselves to produce faith, and I have favored the gospel according to John in this work.

Faith really does come by hearing and hearing by the Word of God, as Paul stated so powerfully in the Roman epistle.

The kind of questions that oftentimes arise are:

- Isn't the Bible full of errors?

- Hasn't science disproved the Bible?

- Doesn't evolution answer all the questions and there remains no longer any need for God?

- Wasn't Jesus just a good moral teacher?

In my view there are nine such questions which come up with regularity, but to give an answer to all of these must be regarded as the subject matter for another book. Unfortunately some Christians regard questions such as those above as offensive, but in the majority of cases, these are genuine questions from honest hearts and puzzled minds that deserve some kind of answer.

Hence these chapters are offered as a minor contribution to giving answers to seeking hearts. It is hoped that they may be helpful in some small way to the marvelous and wonderful business of sharing the gospel in this post Christian world. These reflect discussions I have had with a great many people.

In these chapters we shall be looking at the theme "I Believe Because...". In this world of doubt and atheism, where reasons *not* to believe are presented in the best possible light, where a million pounds spent on a TV series seeking to promote evolutionary theories is commonplace, where atheistic theories and every form of perversion are described as educational programs to encourage enlightenment, there is a great dearth of material available to our young people on why to believe. I thought to attempt to redress this balance a little with a short series on reasons for believing. None of these thoughts should be regarded as presenting the whole picture. Each is a little part of the jigsaw which makes up the evidence for faith.

It is most tragic in our society when we look round and see what happens when man loses God.

- Man the thinker loses his greatest thought...

- Man the worker loses his greatest motive....

- Man the sinner loses his greatest help....

- Man the sufferer loses his greatest comfort....

- Man the mortal loses his only hope.

No wonder the psalmist had this to say:

> *[1] The fool says in his heart, "There is no God."*
> *They are corrupt, they do abominable deeds,*
> *there is none that does good. Psa 14:1*

Doubt, disbelief and distrust have had their day. It is time for us to reply with some answers. Incomplete they may be... but answer we must.

Sigmund Freud the psychiatrist from Vienna in his book "The Future of an Illusion," argues that religion is merely the projection of a wish... and that out there, there is no God. Freud believed that man, because of his fears, developed the idea of a protective father somewhere. That in effect, man created God in his own image rather than the other way around. Through fear of calamity, or crime, man invented God to calm his fears. We would ask, does the fact that man needs God disprove that God exists? The atheist has to prove that God does not exist as much as we need to prove that He does.

I have five children. You might say without fear of contradiction that they need a father, both to guide and protect, as well as to provide for them. Perhaps this seemed more true when they were smaller but even though each of them have made that journey through adolescence to adulthood, they lead me to believe that even now they still like the idea that I am around. They feel a need for a father. Does that mean that therefore I do not exist because I would merely be the product of their wishful thinking? Clearly I do exist. They can see the evidence of this in their lives, in the things I have contributed to them to help them, in the guidance given, in the comfort bestowed, in the relationship experienced. Clearly that is no argument at all. The fact that man needs God does not prove that He does not exist.

Man the technocrat feels he has outgrown his need for God. It seems that there is almost no limit to what man can do. Therefore there is a tendency in the 21st century for man to feel that he is self-sufficient, independent and without any need for God. Man can care for himself and for his every need. Man's pride leads to self-worship. Man makes himself God. Hence far from wishing God into existence that the opposite is true that man is seeking to wish God out of existence. I don't need God's morality. I am God. I will decide my own morality. Hence it is not the believer who is the wishful thinker (wishing God into existence) it is the disbeliever who is the wishful thinker (wishing God out of existence).

There are a large number of arguments we might present and I want to introduce this one thought only here. Some might disagree with it and say it is only an intuitive proof, but it is there nevertheless and should be taken into account. We begin by looking at the nature of man.

> *¹ O LORD, our Lord,*
> *how majestic is thy name in all the earth!*
> *Thou whose glory above the heavens is chanted*
> *² by the mouth of babes and infants,*
> *thou hast founded a bulwark because of thy foes,*
> *to still the enemy and the avenger.*
> *³ When I look at thy heavens, the work of thy fingers,*
> *the moon and the stars which thou hast established;*
> *⁴ what is man that thou art mindful of him,*
> *and the son of man that thou dost care for him?*
> *⁵ Yet thou hast made him little less than God,*
> *and dost crown him with glory and honor.*
> *⁶ Thou hast given him dominion over the works of thy hands;*
> *thou hast put all things under his feet,*
> *⁷ all sheep and oxen,*
> *and also the beasts of the field,*
> *⁸ the birds of the air, and the fish of the sea,*
> *whatever passes along the paths of the sea.*
> *⁹ O LORD, our Lord,*
> *how majestic is thy name in all the earth! Psa 8*

What is man? The Psalmist has posed an interesting question. Is man the product of mere mechanistic evolution or is there something more, something spiritual, something eternal about the nature of man. In looking at man we learn something about the existence of God.

Man's Innate Faith in the Infinite.

Augustine who lived in the fourth and fifth centuries A.D. believed from his own feelings and observations that man has an intuition of the existence of God. There is something about the way that human beings are made that causes us to know that both we, and the universe around us, are products of God. This argument is borne out by modern anthropologists, who would say that man is incurably religious. Wherever man is found, in whatever part of the world, in whatever century, he has been found to be a worshipping creature.

> *22 So Paul, standing in the middle of the Areopagus, said: "Men of Athens, I perceive that in every way you are very religious. 23 For as I passed along, and observed the objects of your worship, I found also an altar with this inscription, 'To an unknown god.' What therefore you worship as unknown, this I proclaim to you. 24 The God who made the world and everything in it, being Lord of heaven and earth, does not live in shrines made by man, 25 nor is he served by human hands, as though he needed anything, since he himself gives to all men life and breath and everything. 26 And he made from one every nation of men to live on all the face of the earth, having determined allotted periods and the boundaries of their habitation, 27 that they should seek God, in the hope that they might feel after him and find him. Yet he is not far from each one of us, 28 for 'In him we live and move and have our being'; as even some of your poets have said, 'For we are indeed his offspring.' Acts 17:22-28*

In every age, in every corner of the globe, men and women have universally believed in the existence of God. They may not always have been very well informed about the nature of God, as in the example above, but they have believed in Him nonetheless.

In around 570 A.D. a group formed a religious community and began to build for themselves a church building, an attempt at a monastic settlement which would one day grow into a cathedral in a dear green place. Today, almost 1500 years later, it is maintained on the same site and the city fathers have a service of blessing for the city council still today in that dear green place that came to be called Glasgow, Scotland's largest city.

In a survey of Scottish churches carried out in October 1994, it was found that 14% of the adult population of Scotland were in church in October 1994. Perhaps some might bemoan that it should have been more. But just think about that for a moment, 14% is an awful lot of people. Were there 14% playing golf, or attending soccer matches? Almost certainly not. The population of Scotland is about 5 million people. If this survey is correct and I have no reason to doubt it, 700,000 people attended church in October of that year. And what is more, if children are included in the survey figures it is 15% of the population attending church. In the Glasgow area, that would amount to 300,000 people attending church on a Sunday.

It is a lesser known fact that in Glasgow, on any weekend during the soccer season, there are more people attend church on a Sunday than attend soccer matches on a Saturday. Think about that for a moment! Is it true that there is a very widespread belief in the existence of God? You better believe it. Christianity is bigger than golf, bigger than soccer, bigger than any sport you care to mention. And whilst attendance figures have fallen in the course of this generation, it is still the biggest game in town. (It is also a fact that numbers attending soccer matches have fallen in this generation too and yet it would be difficult to find anyone predicting the death of soccer.)

Man's Innate Faith in Right or Wrong.

Another interesting aspect of the nature of man is his sense of what we might call "oughtness". Man, no matter how degenerate, has some inborn sense of right and wrong. Even supposing you had never known God and never been taught anything at all about Him, yet it is true that you would still have some sense of what is right and what is wrong.

A cow has no sense of right and wrong. You may recall a case a few years ago reported widely in the press. There was a very prominent British politician called Douglas Hurd. It was reported that his brother was badly savaged and killed by a cow. The cow was not arrested. There was no trial. And there was no talk of a need to restore the death penalty for the cow. Why was that? We recognize that the cow had no ability to make moral judgments. I do not mean to trivialize the seriousness of this tragic accident but the point is well made. Men and cows are treated and regarded differently in law and by all of us.

When a man commits the same crime of killing another man, his treatment is vastly different. We expect better behavior from a man. We expect a man to know that it is not right to kill another person. We might say here that we are discussing something here which is a cousin of conscience though it may well be something more than just conscience. This is a uniquely human quality. Animals do not possess it. It may be part of what the scriptures meant when it said that we are created in the image of God.

> [26] *Then God said, "Let us make man in our image, after our likeness; and let them have dominion over the fish of the sea, and over the birds of the air, and over the cattle, and over all the earth, and over every creeping thing that creeps upon the earth." Gen 1:26*

For God is a free moral agent with choice just like us... and He systematically chooses good all of the time... but He has given us the right to choose right or wrong. God is a moral being and He has given us this inner sense of oughtness.

Paul recognized this in writing to the Romans. His basic message was that all would be justified by faith in Christ or they would not be justified at all. All have sinned and fallen short of the glory of God. The Jews have sinned even though they had the covenants of God. The Gentiles have sinned though they had the evidence of creation. But one might say, that they did not have the law of God so it is not fair that they should be held accountable for disobeying a law they never knew. Note carefully how Paul answers this point:

> *[14] When Gentiles who have not the law do by nature what the law requires, they are a law to themselves, even though they do not have the law. [15] They show that what the law requires is written on their hearts, while their conscience also bears witness and their conflicting thoughts accuse or perhaps excuse them [16] on that day when, according to my gospel, God judges the secrets of men by Christ Jesus.   Rom 2:14-16*

Those who never knew the Law of Moses would not be judged by that law which they never had the opportunity to know, but would be judged on the basis of the law they did know, that law which was within them, that sense of right and wrong which was within them because they were created in the image of a moral God.

Theoretically of course, it is possible according to this teaching for man not to sin... i.e. if he lives up perfectly even to a rudimentary ethical code which is his own. Yet in practice there is not a person alive or in history who has ever successfully lived up to his own view of morality one hundred percent successfully. Inevitably we all violate this sense of right conduct. When a man does this he becomes a sinner and is lost. His only hope then is to be saved by faith in Christ, be being obedient to the gospel of Christ. Hence Jesus could say...

> *"I am the way, and the truth, and the life; no one comes to the Father, but by me.   Jn 14:6*

C.S. Lewis was a great exponent of this in his book "Mere Christianity". He comments that it is oft heard that men make statements like...

- How'd you like it if anyone did the same to you?
- Leave him alone he isn't doing you any harm.
- Give me a bit of your chocolate, I gave you a bit of mine.

People say things like that every day and when they do it is clear that they are appealing to some kind of standard of behavior which he expects the other man to know about. It looks as if both parties had in mind some kind of Law or Rule of fair play, decent behavior or morality. He goes on to suggest that this is a worldwide phenomenon and that there is no society in which selfishness is admired, or where man feels proudest of double-crossing his neighbor. Men have differed as to whether you might have one wife or four, but they have always agreed that you must not simply have any woman you liked. There are in fact two fundamental observations we might make:

1. Human beings all over the earth have this curious idea that they ought to behave in a certain way and cannot easily get rid of it.

2. They do not in reality behave in that way.

Some time back there was a real life drama on TV, reconstructing an amazing event. A little boy, three years old, had wandered off from home with his dog. He had gone off into a disused dock when the tide was out and was stuck up to his chest in mud. The dog remained beside him barking and attracting attention. Three workmen spotted the dog and then the boy. They threw lumber and other materials found around the dock on to the uncertain surface until they could, by hanging on to big tires and lumps of wood make their way out to the boy and pull him free. He was rescued and eventually brought him back to safety. The men were later given an award for bravery, and the dog won the admiration of everyone who heard about it. Imagine yourself in the same position. Two instincts or impulses immediately register themselves.

a. the desire to plunge into the dock and save the child.

b. the desire to avoid danger and not risk one's own life.

But you will find inside you a third impulse which tells you that

c. you ought to go and help the child.

If there are only two impulses, then it is the stronger one which will win and the weaker one which will lose. It is at these moments of decision that we are most conscious of the fact that the sense of right and wrong, the sense of oughtness placed in us by God appeals to us to side with the perhaps weaker impulse and do what is right.

Thomas B. Warren in his debates with Anthony Flew and Wallace Matson on the existence of God makes a wonderfully valid point. He asked his opponents to consider the holocaust, when the Nazis murdered 6 million Jews. And he posed them the question, was this right or wrong?

If they were to answer that they believed that the Nazis had done wrong, they were then asked should they be tried, and ultimately punished for that wrong. And if the answer to that is in the affirmative, under what law should they be tried, what law had they broken? The problem was that they were not violating German law and they were clearly not under British law. So what law had they violated that they should be tried?

The Nazis maintained that they had the right to protect their society and protect their master race from the Jews and the Gypsies, and if there had been many black Germans at that time no doubt they would have been included also. Their law not only permitted but commanded them to exterminate these threats. The Nazi defense went something like this:

1. Our society had its own needs and desires.

2. Our society made its own laws, based on those needs and desires.

3. Our society commanded us to exterminate the Jews.

4. It would have been wrong for us not to have obeyed.

5. Now you try to condemn us by the law of an alien society... a value system which has nothing to do with Nazi philosophy and law.

The accusers said something like this.....

1. We appeal to a higher law which rises above the provincial and the transient.

   R. H. Jackson (Closing Address in the Nuremberg trial)

Conclusion:

Much more could be said about the nature of man. For we have said nothing about the evidence of design in man. Many writers have waxed eloquent on these points and I have no desire to pursue this further in this chapter. I simply want to concentrate on two points in this lesson, these two points and no others.

a) **That there is universal belief in God in mankind.**
Where did that belief come from? Did man invent God because he needs Him or is there some other explanation? Rather, man who is made in the image of God is incomplete without a relationship with the eternal and infinite God. Man instinctively seeks after the God who made him. Some have said that the beast walks around on four legs with its eyes turned towards the ground. Man walks on two legs with his eyes turned heavenward.

b) **That there is a universal sense of morality in man.**
This morality is not always in detailed agreement but it is always there. Sometimes this morality or conscience requires education as in the case of Saul of Tarsus, but even the heathen who has never read the Bible has a sense of morality that he attempts to live by. Where did that sense of morality come from? If man is some cosmic accident, how can an amoral mechanistic universe create a moral man? Surely it is the case that man is a moral being, a moral agent who makes moral choices and that he is made in the image of a moral God.

For these reasons amongst many others, I believe in God.

Man without God is without purpose or direction... he has no reason for existence and a sense of emptiness within for he is cut off from the eternal God who made him and gives him the sense of fulfillment. Man without God is left with the feeling that he should behave in certain ways without really being able to understand or explain why. He finds his why in God. I believe in God because of the nature of man.

Chapter Fourteen.

I Believe Because... The Bible!!

BECAUSE THERE ARE MANY REASONS for believing, these chapters can only be short indications of arguments that may help us to see that it is not necessary to ditch coherent and logical thought in order to believe in the gospel and become a disciple of Jesus. Among the reasons for believing is the nature of the Bible.

The Bible stands alone as the world's most amazing book. The tragedy is that in our society it has become a treasure in the dust. For it lies unopened and unread in the majority of homes and even in many churches throughout the land. We want to remind ourselves and our friends and neighbors just how remarkable and wonderful is the Word of God. It becomes, in and of itself a reason for believing.

The Bible Claims to be the Word of God:

First of all we should note that the Bible makes some remarkable claims for itself. It does not view itself as any ordinary book. Notice how the Bible speaks about the process of its own production:-

> *All Scripture is inspired by God and profitable for teaching, for reproof, for correction, and for training in righteousness, that the man of God may be complete, equipped for every good work.*   *2 Tim 3:16-17.*

Notice carefully what is being said here. Scripture is inspired. This is a word we throw around very loosely today. We talk about Shakespeare being an inspired writer, or Milton an inspired poet, or some over paid, over rated footballer being an inspired player. But this is to devalue the word used in this passage. The literal word used is *Theopneustos*. This in English would be "God-breathed". It means that in the same way that God breathed the breath of life into man at the creation, so God breathed this Word. It comes from the impetus of God, it springs from Him not man.

And hence that Word is profitable to man. It claims that it is profitable to be taught to man. It claims that it is profitable to **reprove** man wherein he has done wrong. Further it is profitable to **train** man in righteous living. It should also be noted that the passage claims that this Word is that which **equips** man for good living and also that which **makes man complete** and thus he finds his fulfillment in the Word of God. It claims a good deal for itself. It does not proclaim "read me as you would read any other book."... "read me for the sake of curing your curiosity".. "read me as you would the newspaper."

It demands our attention. It commands our respect. It calls for complete obedience to its teaching. And Why? Because it claims to be nothing less than God-breathed, the Word of God. We note a further passage of Scripture.

> *First of all you must understand this, that no prophecy of Scripture is a matter of one's own interpretation, because no prophecy ever came by the impulse of man, but men moved by the Holy Spirit spoke from God. 2 Pet 1:20-21.*

The statements of these verses are worth very close scrutiny. We note that the Bible is not to be used as so many use it today... as a proof text to prove every unbelievable and strange doctrine under the sun. Have you heard people say, "You can prove anything by the Bible". And that may be true if you treat it as many people treat it. But if you are going to misuse the Bible and take it out of context and twist its meaning as Peter warned against, then what you have at the end of it is not the Word of God at all, but merely the assorted words of men. No statement of Scripture, no prophecy can be mistreated in that way for it is not just man's word. It is God's Word and should be treated with respect.

Further we might point out that the words used suggest something about the mechanism for inspiration, a matter which is under constant debate. Men moved by the Holy Spirit spoke from God.

a) Note firstly that it was the men that spoke. God did not use them as word processors or typewriters but He employed them as men to speak. This means that each man retained his own linguistic style and vocabulary and confirms what we find in a study of the Bible, that each writer did indeed have his own style. It was verbal inspiration... but not in the sense that God dictated to each writer each word to be written. But it was verbal in the sense that God so controlled each man that each word that he wrote was the very word that God wanted him to write.

b) The word moved implies control. Indeed it is the same word used in Acts 27 to speak of how the ship Paul was shipwrecked on was carried along by the great storm and wind. That small ship had no choice... had no control in the matter. It was borne along by the mighty wind. So also here, we learn that the writers of Scripture were borne along by the Holy Spirit and wrote just what God wanted them to write.

The Bible claims a unique position in all literature, it claims to be the very word of God, inspired, God-breathed.. and as such demands our attention, our reverence, our obedience.

The Bible Shows itself to be the Word of God.

We would go further and say that not only does the Bible claim to be the Word of God, it shows itself to be the Word of God. The problem with so many people today is not that they have read the Bible and found it to be wanting. It is that they have never read it at all.

Among the evidences concerning the Bible is the existence of Scientific Foreknowledge in the writings of the Bible. This shows that the Bible is something beyond the knowledge and experiences of mere man. We do not find the superstitions and wrong notions concerning scientific matters which were current in the ancient world in which the Scriptures were written.

How easy it would have been for Moses to have slipped at one point or another by including such things as then believed hypotheses that the earth was flat and rested upon the back of some great turtle or elephant. The most natural thing in the world would have been for these ancient writers to include many of these superstitions in the Bible which later would have been proved false. The absence of these things is impressive evidence that God must have guided and superintended these writers. Let us notice a few examples:

1. Job 26:7

> *He stretches out the north over the void, and hangs the earth upon nothing.*

We have watched the pictures of the earth from space and it is entirely obvious that the earth is hung on nothing and is riding free in space. But how would ancient Job have known this, living centuries ago, before the time of Moses. One theory was that the earth was balanced on the back of a giant turtle swimming in some giant sea in a larger world. You might ask, what was that world suspended on? It was on the back of an even bigger turtle. And guess what, that's right, it's turtles all the way down.

Job never said that! He declared that the earth was hanging on nothing... as if he had somehow caught a glimpse of the Apollo TV pictures.... technology he could never begin to dream of.

2. Isa 40:22.

> *It is he who sits above the circle of the earth, and its*
> *inhabitants are like grasshoppers; who stretches out the heavens*
> *like a curtain. and spreads them like a tent to dwell in.*

How did Isaiah come to describe the earth as a circle... or the word can be translated orb... the earth as a ball hanging on nothing in space. This is pretty advanced scientific knowledge... far beyond the ancient world in which these books were written. Indeed if such things had been written 2000 years later they would have been snubbed as fanciful. But here they are in the pages of the ancient Bible.

3. Psa 8:1-9.

> *¹ O LORD, our Lord,*
> *how majestic is thy name in all the earth!*
> *Thou whose glory above the heavens is chanted ² by the*
> *mouth of babes and infants,*
> *thou hast founded a bulwark because of thy foes,*
> *to still the enemy and the avenger.*
> *³ When I look at thy heavens, the work of thy fingers,*
> *the moon and the stars which thou hast established;*
> *⁴ what is man that thou art mindful of him,*
> *and the son of man that thou dost care for him?*
> *⁵ Yet thou hast made him little less than God,*
> *and dost crown him with glory and honor.*
> *⁶ Thou hast given him dominion over the works of thy*
> *hands;*
> *thou hast put all things under his feet,*
> *⁷ all sheep and oxen,*
> *and also the beasts of the field,*
> *⁸ the birds of the air, and the fish of the sea,*
> *whatever passes along the paths of the sea.*
> *⁹ O LORD, our Lord,*
> *how majestic is thy name in all the earth!*

Matthew Fontaine Maury was ill one day and was having his son read to him from the Bible. His son read these lines to him from the eighth Psalm. Maury stopped his son and asked him to read the 8th verse again. Then he stated that if the Word of God says there are paths in the sea they must be there, and I will find them. Within a few years he had charted the primary paths or currents of the oceans which are still followed by ocean going vessels to this day! How did the author of this psalm know about the "paths of the sea" before scientists knew of them, especially when we remember that Israel was not renowned as a sea-going nation.

4. Jer 33:22.

> [22] *As the host of heaven cannot be numbered and the sands of the sea cannot be measured, so I will multiply the descendants of David my servant, and the Levitical priests who minister to me."*

How many stars are there? The ancients thought that there were a relatively small finite number. The fact of the vast host of stars is in fact a modern discovery. Hipparchus, about a century and a half before Christ gave the number of stars as 1022 and Ptolemy in the beginning of the second century could find 1026. We may on a clear night with the unaided eye see only 1060, or, if we could survey the whole celestial sphere about 3000. But with the invention of the telescope around 300 years ago by Galileo, then for the first time men began to know that Jeremiah was right when he made the stars as countless as the sand on the seashore.

5. Job 28:25.

> [25] *When he gave to the wind its weight,*
> *and meted out the waters by measure;*

Note how Job speaks of giving wind its weight. i.e. giving the atmosphere or breath weight. The idea that even air has weight was not something that would have occurred to the ancients. We can measure that weight in the science lab today... by pumping out a flask, weighing it before- filled with air and weighing it after, we can establish the weight of the air in the flask. The weight in the atmosphere was not known till the time of Galileo. But Job knew!

6. Luke 17:31-36.

> [31] *On that day, let him who is on the housetop, with his goods in the house, not come down to take them away;*

and likewise let him who is in the field not turn back. ³² Remember Lot's wife. ³³ Whoever seeks to gain his life will lose it, but whoever loses his life will preserve it. ³⁴ I tell you, in that night there will be two in one bed; one will be taken and the other left. ³⁵ There will be two women grinding together; one will be taken and the other left."

In this passage the time of the coming of the Lord is discussed. When shall that moment be? The Bible tells us that we cannot know that date but that we should make sure that we are ready for His coming. In these verses we note that in v31 the scene being presented is a daytime scene. There are those who are working in the field. This has to be during the day. However in v34 it is most definitely a night-time scene. Hence as we look at what the Bible has to say about the time when the Lord shall return and all shall be heralded into our eternal destiny... there are some who will experience it during the day and some who will experience it at night. How can that be? Unless of course we take into account that in this world of ours there are places where it is day and at exactly the same moment it is night on another part of the globe. Simultaneously it is both night and day at the same moment depending on where you are in the earth at that very time. This presupposes that we understand that the earth is a great ball and the sun shines on one side of that ball at a time. How could the New Testament writers know these things? How could Jesus, raised in a village in ancient Palestine know these things?

Yes, it might be said that the Bible has demonstrated that it is no ordinary book but has shown itself to be the very word of God.

The Bible Has Proved Itself to be the Word of God.

Finally we want to state that the Bible not only claims to be the Word of God, not only has it shown itself to be the Word of God, it has proved itself to be the Word of God because of fulfilled prophecy.

The Bible itself makes it clear that fulfilled prophecy is a sign of inspiration... if the prophet's words do not come true... do not listen to the prophet.

15 "The LORD your God will raise up for you a prophet like me from among you, from your brethren—him you shall heed— 16 just as you desired of the LORD your God at Horeb on the day of the assembly, when you said, 'Let me not hear again the voice of the LORD my God, or see this great fire any more, lest I die.' 17 And the LORD said to me, 'They have rightly said all that they have spoken. 18 I will raise up for them a prophet like you from among their brethren; and I will put my words in his mouth, and he shall speak to them all that I command him. 19 And whoever will not give heed to my words which he shall speak in my name, I myself will require it of him. 20 But the prophet who presumes to speak a word in my name which I have not commanded him to speak, or who speaks in the name of other gods, that same prophet shall die.' 21 And if you say in your heart, 'How may we know the word which the LORD has not spoken?' — 22 when a prophet speaks in the name of the LORD, if the word does not come to pass or come true, that is a word which the LORD has not spoken; the prophet has spoken it presumptuously, you need not be afraid of him. Deut 18:15-22

In this prophecy of the coming of the Christ... we see this principle being put forward... if the prophet's words do not come true, then this is not a prophet of God, his words do not come from God.

There are literally hundreds of examples of fulfilled prophecies of the Bible...showing without a shadow of doubt that the Bible prophets spoke from God.

The Bible predicted the downfall of nations or cities... and the prophecies were shown to be true. Prosperous Tyre was left without one stone upon another.[9] The Edomites would be destroyed.[10] Israel would be conquered and carried off into captivity in Babylon.[11] Then the Bible predicts their return after 70 years under the edict of a certain

---

[9] See Ezek 26:1-6.
[10] The book of Obadiah.
[11] Micah 4:10.

King Cyrus not yet born and hence not yet named by his mother... and to rebuild the city and the temple.[12]

A most cursory glance at just one prophecy is instructive. Suppose we were to look at the prophecy contained in Daniel ch 2 and the great vision of Nebuchadnezzar. In Daniel ch 2 the king has a dream and he commands his wise men and his advisors to tell him first what was in the dream and second what it meant. The second would be difficult but a man clever in words could dream something up. The first was of course impossible. But Daniel with the help of God was equal to both tasks. The king saw a great figure in his dream and the figure was made up of different materials. (Dan 2:31-35) Then in v36ff we see that Daniel goes on to interpret the dream.

Each of the materials represented a different world empire. The Babylonian empire was represented by the head of gold. But the king was warned by Daniel that the empire would soon fall and would be replaced by another. The breast and arms of silver would represent an inferior kingdom. Thus history and the Word of God confirms was the Medo-Persian empire. Darius the Mede was to ascend the throne. But that kingdom too was to fall to a yet inferior kingdom represented by the belly and thighs of bronze. History tells us that this represented the empire of Alexander the Great (Greek) and his successors. Finally the legs and feet of iron mixed with clay would represent a very powerful kingdom... but a kingdom with weakness mixed in (clay). This represented the Roman Empire.

Then in v44 Daniel makes this vital prophecy. In the days of those kings (i.e. the Roman kingdom) there would be set up a kingdom which would never be destroyed. And that kingdom was the church of our Lord. He ascended the throne in the days of the Roman Empire and He rules still. And so in every respect the prophetic statements of Daniel were found to be true.

But the most striking of the prophecies of the Old Testament were those concerning the coming Messiah... what his parentage should be..

---

[12] Isa 44:28ff. These prophecies some 150 years or more before the event
predict the return of the Jews from captivity and rebuilding of the temple
of God in Jerusalem.

where he should be born... that He might be born of a virgin... where His ministry would be found (by the sea of Galilee)... the nature of His ministry... His triumphal entry into Jerusalem... His crucifixion... His rising from the dead. All of these things were predicted... over 300 predictions concerning the person and ministry of the Christ were fulfilled in Jesus.

Prophecy	Fulfillment
1 Of the tribe of Judah (Gen 49:10)	Luke 3:23-38
2 Of royal line of David (Jer 23:5)	Matt 1:1
3 Born of a virgin (Isa 7:14)	Matt 1:18-25
4 Born in Bethlehem (Micah 5:2)	Matt 2:1-6 [13]
5 Infants slaughtered to try to kill him (Jer 31:15)	Matt 2:16-18
6 A forerunner would prepare the way (Mal 3:1)	Matt 3:1-2
7 Focus of ministry in Galilee (Isa 9:1-2)	Matt 4:11-16
8 Shall enter Jerusalem riding on an ass (Zech 9:9)	Matt 21:6-7
9 Be betrayed by a disciple (Psa 41:9)	Matt 26:14-15
10 Betrayal price predicted (Zech 11:12)	Matt 27:3-7
11 Betrayal money to be returned (Zech 11:13)	Matt 27:3-7
12 He shall suffer in silence (Isa 53:7)	Matt 27:12-14
13 His hands and feet would be pierced (Psa 22:16)	Luke 23:33
14 They divided his garments (Psa 22:18)	John 19:23-24
15 He would be spat upon (Isa 50:6)	Mark 14:65
16 Not a bone would be broken (Psa 34:20)	John 19:33-36
17 He shall be pierced (Zech 12:10)	John 19:33-37
18 Be buried with the rich (Isa 53:9)	Matt 27:57-60
19 Would rise from the dead (Psa 16:10)	Matt 28:6, Acts 2:22-32
20 When Son came, God came (Isa 9:6-9)	John 1:1-14

---

[13] Note that it took a decree from Augustus Caesar to fulfil this prophecy... the decree meant that Mary and Joseph had to return to their ancestral home city, the city of David, Bethlehem and it was there that the Christ was born.

It has been estimated that there are over 300 prophecies of the Christ which are fulfilled in Jesus and the above is only meant to be a taster of the enormous weight of evidence concerning Jesus which establish His validity as the promised Messiah. And many of these details were outwith His ability to artificially fulfill. One cannot govern one's place of birth, nor how others will treat you, nor where you will be buried following your death. Nor can one determine the price that will be paid to your betrayer. But all of these details were predicted hundreds of years before the event.

And hence we see without a doubt that the Bible has shown itself to be a supernatural book, inspired of God, and deserving of our attention and our obedience.

Conclusion.

What are the odds of making all the prophecies of Scripture be fulfilled by chance or accident? Is it possible that this is all some coincidental fulfillment of prophecy.

Let us suppose that the chance of a prophecy being true or not is 1/2. i.e. one chance in two, it is either true or it is not. In fact many prophecies would be a lot less likely than that, but we shall be conservative. Suppose then instead of the hundreds involved there were just 25 fulfilled prophecies. Then the mathematical probability of all 25 being fulfilled would be as follows:-

1 chance in 2^{25}

i.e. 1 chance in two to the power 25. Or 2x2x2x2x ... (25 times the number two will appear) or 1 chance in 33,554,432.

And that is just if there is an even chance of the prophecy being fulfilled by chance. Of course some of the events are a lot less likely than that. What do you think the odds are against a baby being born without a human father?

But the odds are at most one in 33 million against the Bible accidentally fulfilling just 25 prophecies.

I believe Because......
I believe because of the supernatural character of the Bible.

Chapter Fifteen

I Believe Because…The Universal Law of Cause and Effect

THERE ARE INDEED MANY REASONS for believing in God and Christ, and in each of these chapters we are only touching on some of the most common arguments that have been put forward through the years.

In this particular lesson, we shall be turning to what has been called the Law of Cause and Effect. The argument is indeed a simple one.

1. No effect can be produced without a cause.

2. The world and everything in it, is an effect! What is the cause?

Our world exists within a universe. In our world are living things like flowers, trees, birds, cows and human beings. Where did all these things come from? It is axiomatic that nothing comes from nothing. If there had been a time when nothing existed, then without intervention nothing would exist today. But life is here now; therefore it must have had an origin. Life must have come from something or someone.

Have you ever walked along a beach first thing in the morning right after the tide has gone out? Perhaps you are walking along the beach and you look down and see that there are footprints in the sand stretching out before you. You look ahead into the distance but you can see no one. Indeed you have never seen anyone that morning at all.

Yet you know with an absolute certainty in your heart that someone walked along here before you. You never saw them. Yet you believe it with certainty. Because footprints don't come from nowhere. They cannot arrive from nothing. So it goes with our universe. We cannot prove in a scientific way that there is a God who made it, but we know that it is certainly true because it is there.

When Benjamin Franklin was Ambassador of the United Nations to France, he was a member of an elite literary social and scientific club. At certain of the meetings of this intellectual group, atheistic sentiments were expressed leaving the impression that only the superstitious and uninformed still believed in God as the creator of the universe. At the next meeting of the group Benjamin Franklin brought a beautifully designed and executed model of the sun and our entire solar system. The earth and the other planets were in their proper relationship to the sun and each other and of appropriate sizes. It was a masterpiece. Upon seeing it, one of the sophisticated members of the club asked, "Who made it?" Dryly and without a trace of a smile, Franklin responded, "No one. It just happened."

The writer to the Hebrews was well familiar with this kind of argument for we note these words from the third chapter:

For every house is built by some one, but the builder of all things is God.

Just as when we go out for a walk, and we come upon a house in the woods, we might not know who built it, but of one thing we are absolutely certain, we know that someone did. Bricklayers laid those bricks. Joiners worked on those rafters and joists, plumbers put in the pipes and electricians wired the electrics. In the same way, we must conclude that there was a builder for this universal house we inhabit.

Dr Edward Luther Kessel said, *"Science clearly shows that the universe could not have existed from all eternity. The law of entropy states that there is a continuous flow of heat from warmer to cooler bodies... Therefore the universe is headed for a time when the temperature will be universally uniform and there will be no more useful energy. Consequently there will be no more chemical or physical processes, and life itself will cease to exist. But because life is still going and chemical and physical processes are still in progress it is evident that our universe could not have existed from eternity, else it would have long since run out of useful energy and ground to a halt. Therefore quite unintentionally, science proves that our universe had a beginning. And in doing so it proves the reality of God, for whatever had a beginning did not begin of itself but demands a Prime Mover, a Creator, a God."*

Dr Merritt Stanley Congdon, a natural scientist wrote, *"Without exception, we find that 'Nothing comes from nothing.' Are we to believe that the universe in its entirety is an exception to this universal law? Whatever force it is that brought our universe into being, we call God."*

Frank Allen, a biophysicist commented that there are four possible solutions of the origin of the universe:

1. It is an illusion.

2. It spontaneously arose out of nothing.

3. It had no origin but existed eternally.

4. It was created.

The first is playing with philosophy and probably needs little comment. It suggests that there are illusory buses filled with imaginary people passing along this street, and theoretical cars traveling through an unreal tunnel under a postulated river, traveling to imaginary houses in imagined housing schemes for there is no real world at all but we imagine it. At least I do, I'm not really sure if you exist or you are just a figment of my imagination.

The second suggests that the world of matter arose spontaneously out of nothing. This is against every known or observed law in the universe. And hence we need to say little about it.

The third will not be allowed by the known laws of Physics. The second law of thermodynamics tells us that the universe is running down to a condition when all bodies will be at the same extremely low temperature and no energy will be available. Life will then be impossible. If the universe was eternal, then this state would long ago have been reached. The fact that this is not the case indicates that the origin of the universe occurred in time, at a fixed point in time and therefore the universe must have been created.

No wonder, Lord Kelvin, the noted scientist of Glasgow University, after whom the Kelvin temperature scale and Kelvingrove Park in Glasgow are named made the following significant statement:

"If you think strongly enough, you will be forced by Science to believe in God.

Indeed, although popular belief might suggest the opposite, there are many in the scientific world who do believe in a Creator God, and of the most significant scientists of the past, a great many of them believed in God.

I recently wrote an article and sent it off to one of the religious papers in the hope it will be published. The article was based on a piece of research conducted in 1996 repeating a piece of research which had been done 80 years earlier. The idea was essentially a simple one: Do scientists believe in God and an afterlife? The research in 1916 took 1000 names from the Who's Who of American Science and sent them all a questionnaire. They were asked whether they believed in God or not. (And the question was quite specific... did they believe in a God who hears and answers prayer?) In 1916 the results were regarded as something quite shocking for it was found that only 40% of the scientists believed in God. There was much debate at the time concerning this shocking research. Would science wipe out belief in God? A new study was done in 1996 repeating the exercise as exactly as possible. What would 80 years of scientific research have done to belief in God? The results would be tantalizing. The same procedures were followed as before. 100 scientists were selected and the same wording was used. The findings were that some 40% of the scientists believed in God. No change. Further research taken in America shows that some 40% of the general population in America also believe in God. Hence being a scientist or not makes no difference to faith in God. They were no more likely and no less likely to choose to believe in God than anyone else in society.

The work of the scientist could be described as seeking out and trying to understand the order that it is in the universe. It is true that there is a universe here to be studied, but where did it come from?

We have a universe here which is not a haphazard universe ruled by chance, how did it arise?

Chemistry Declares God Is.

A hundred years ago it was the Russian scientist Mendeleev who identified the various arrangements of the substances we identify as elements, i.e. substances which cannot be reduced further. He first identified the chemical elements in order of increasing atomic weight into what is referred to as the Periodic Table. Not only did this lead to formulating various laws and relationships concerning the atomic characteristics of the elements, it also led to being able to predict the existence and properties of certain elements which up until that time were undiscovered. He predicted their existence and almost exactly the properties they would have.

Why? Why is there such order in this world if it is truly a world of chance and happenstance? The existence of these elements, their very predictability shows that there is an ordered Mind behind it all, who designed and made it according to His design.

Elmer Maurer who was a research chemist wrote these words concerning the periodic table of elements:

> *"If I were to walk into the forest and suddenly find a*
> *clearing with a cozy cottage surrounded by flowers and*
> *beautiful shrubbery. It would seem ridiculous to me to say*
> *that they just happened. And so it is with the elements,*
> *and the periodic chart, and all the laws of nature. Simple*
> *logic requires that somebody planned them, and made and*
> *established them. To me this planner and maker is God.*

Physics Declares that God Is.

As a physicist, the whole of my study has been concerned with the examination of all the evidences of order in the universe. Whenever we find one of the unvarying patterns, we describe that as a law of the universe, or a law of physics. But physicists don't write laws, don't invent them, they simply discover the ones that are already in existence. The physicist notes that two bodies who have mass attract each other, and we call that the law of gravitational attraction. It is that law which means that anything we drop always goes down the way and not up. How two bodies attract each other is well described in Newton's Law of Gravitation, but why they do is not known.

There is an accepted law governing the forces between electrically charged bodies, whether positive or negative. The law states that the force is one of attraction if the charges are of the opposite sign and of repulsion if of the same sign, the force in either case being proportional to the product of the two charges and inversely proportional to the square of the separation distance. Why this should be so, we do not know, but we know that it is always so, except in some very special circumstances where we believe there are some other very special strong forces present.

Some would point to the Big Bang Theory as the answer to the origin of the universe. But even that theory is no answer at all. For if the universe came from a highly compressed, very hot beginning it would still not explain where those very hot compressed gases came from. God would still be in the picture.

When I studied the Second Law of Thermodynamics in my second year of a Physics degree, the lecture was introduced by the words, "Today we are going to study the second law of thermodynamics and we do not wish to enter into any discussion on the philosophical implications of this law." I did not have a clue what he was on about. Why had he made that statement? The law can be quite complicated however it can be understood by anyone at a fairly basic level. It is concerned with the idea of a quality called entropy. It in essence is the degree of disorder in the universe. And it has been noted that every transaction that takes place leads to greater and greater entropy. The universe is going from a more ordered to a less ordered state every day. There is less and less energy available to us. We might illustrate this as follows:

Suppose we had three inter-connecting rooms. One room we heated up to 100°F, a second room we left at a cool 60°F and the third we refrigerated down to 4°F. If we opened the doors between the rooms, what would happen? We know that heat would flow from the hottest to the others until eventually all three rooms were at the same temperature and heat would not flow any more. Note the implications of this to the universe. There are hot stars like the sun and cooler planets and the planets are receiving heat from the suns. This tells us something.... the universe is not infinitely old. If it were infinitely old, everything would be at the same temperature and there would not be any hot spots any more. By this law of physics, we see that it is proved that the universe had a beginning and if it had a beginning, then it suggests that it has an Originator. No material thing can create itself.

Another similar argument can be made from geology. In a universe which had no beginning, but had always existed, no radioactive elements would remain, all would have decayed. The fact that radioactivity exists points to a finite universe created at a specific time in history.

The concept of a cyclical universe alternately expanding and contracting is extra-scientific, it is an unproved hypothesis, or if you like, sheer guesswork. In fact, at this time of writing, it has been noted that instead of the rate of expansion of the universe slowing, heading towards a reversal and implosion of the universe, the rate of expansion is speeding up. This would tend to disprove this hypothesis.

The more I studied and learned about Physics, the more impressed I was with the order and symmetry of the laws of Physics. I once sat in a research seminar concerning the fundamental particles of the universe. The latest research confirmed that all of the known universe is made up of exactly four symmetrically arranged families of particles. And the latest research believes that there will be these four and only these four and no others are to be found. The researcher said there were two very interesting fundamental questions to be answered. How many fundamental particles, in how many families? And, secondly, if that is so, why are there only these and not an infinite variety? He spent a couple of hours on the first question and ran out of time before approaching the second. The answer is, science does not have a clue to any questions beginning with why?

Seemingly unrelated phenomena have a common form. If we compare the laws of gravitational attraction, magnetic attraction and electrostatic attraction, the laws have an extremely close similarity in appearance. It is as if the laws of Physics were built by the same designer, and built well for the laws are always obeyed... the intricate design was faithfully built according to the Divine blueprint.

The prophet Isaiah made a statement some 700 years before Christ which seems to be very apt here:

> [18] *For thus says the LORD, who created the heavens (he is*
> *God!), who formed the earth and made it (he established it;*
> *he did not create it a chaos, he formed it to be inhabited!):*
> *"I am the LORD, and there is no other. Isa 45:18*

The principle or law of causality is fundamental to all physicists. Perhaps the father of modern physics is Isaac Newton. His fundamental laws of physics postulated in the 1600's are still taught as the basis of physics today. Newton's first law may be stated as this:

> *A body which is at rest will continue to remain at rest, or*
> *a body in uniform motion will continue in that uniform*
> *motion unless a force acts upon it.*

You might say that that is really obvious. But until Newton had formulated this in his Principia Mathematica in the 1600's no one had figured it out before. You might paraphrase that and say that nothing happens without a cause. If things don't change they will remain the same. This is the whole point. No universe would come into being unless someone, some thing, some force, some creative force brings it into being.

Biology Declares God Is.

A fundamental law of biology may be referred to as the law of biogenesis. When we think of the living cell, we might wonder how this microscopic but amazing functional unit came into being. How was it set in motion? We are confronted with formidable even insuperable difficulties in trying to account for its beginning. It has been noted again and again that it is an undeniable law that life only springs from life. If that be true, how did the first living cells come into being. That is a question which even now cannot be satisfactorily answered.

Professor Edwin Conklin, who was a biologist at Princeton University has said, *"The probability of life originating by accident is comparable to the probability of the Unabridged Dictionary resulting from an explosion in a printing shop."*

Conclusion:

As we have seen with this very brief survey of what certain scientists have said and what certain scientific laws demand, it is simply just not the case that science is slowly but surely disproving the Bible and man no longer needs to believe in the existence of God. Rather one very reasonable point of view is that the opposite is true and that science is slowly but surely driving man back to God. The more we learn of the truth, the more we shall appreciate the greatness of our Creator.

Paul pointed out a long time ago that the world around us is eloquent testimony to the creator God.

> *For the wrath of God is revealed from heaven against all ungodliness and wickedness of men who by their wickedness suppress the truth. For what can be known about God is plain to them, because God has shown it to them. Ever since the creation of the world his invisible nature, namely, his eternal power and deity, has been clearly perceived in the things that have been made. So they are without excuse; for although they knew God they did not honor him as God or give thanks to him, but they became futile in their thinking and their senseless minds were darkened. Claiming to be wise, they became fools. Rom 1:18-22.*

The evidence is there to be seen, in Chemistry, in Physics, in Biology... that God is the great Designer and Creator. His invisible Deity and power are seen clearly in things that He has made.

Some 1000 years earlier than Paul's writing, the psalmist had made essentially the same point:

> *O LORD, our Lord, how majestic is thy name in all the earth! Thou whose glory above the heavens is chanted by the mouth of babes and infants, thou hast founded a bulwark because of thy foes, to still the enemy and the avenger. When I look at thy heavens, the work of thy fingers, the moon*

and the stars which thou hast established; what is man that thou art mindful of him, and the son of man that thou dost care for him? Yet thou hast made him little less than God, and dost crown him with glory and honor. Thou hast given him dominion over the works of thy hands; thou hast put all things under his feet, all sheep and oxen, and also the beasts of the field, the birds of the air, and the fish of the sea, whatever passes along the paths of the sea. O LORD, our Lord, how majestic is thy name in all the earth! Psa 8

and again

The heavens are telling the glory of God; and the firmament proclaims his handiwork. Day to day pours forth speech, and night to night declares knowledge. There is no speech, nor are there words; their voice is not heard; yet their voice goes out through all the earth, and their words to the end of the world. In them he has set a tent for the sun, which comes forth like a bridegroom leaving his chamber, and like a strong man runs its course with joy. Its rising is from the end of the heavens, and its circuit to the end of them; and there is nothing hid from its heat. Psa 19:1-6

Whether we gaze at the heavens and the expanding universe with its definite beginning, or we somehow peer into the intricacies of the atom and its subatomic particles and see the marvelous order and evidence of design, we agree with the psalmist of so long ago: *The heavens are telling the glory of God; and the firmament proclaims His handiwork.*

Chapter Sixteen

I Believe Because.... Miracles

IN ANY EXAMINATION OF THE field of Christian evidences, reasons for believing, it is necessary to include a consideration of miracles. What do we mean by miracles? One dictionary definition is, "an event or effect in the physical world deviating from the known laws of nature, or transcending our knowledge of these laws: a wonder or wonderful thing; a marvel." (Webster's New Collegiate Dictionary) C.S. Lewis defined a miracle as "an interference with Nature by supernatural power." The Westminster Dictionary of the Bible gives an even better definition: "Miracles are events in the external world, wrought by the immediate power of God and intended as a sign or attestation".

Often in John's gospel these miracles are referred to as signs. This again emphasizes that they had a purpose. They are not just wondrous events, worthy of discussion... but they are meant to signify something. They were signs pointing towards something... in this case the deity of the Christ.

> *Now Jesus did many other signs in the presence of the*
> *disciples which are not written in this book; but these are*
> *written that you may believe that Jesus is the Christ, the Son*
> *of God, and that believing you may have life in His name.*
> *Jn 20:30-31*

Some people of course have problems with the miracles. They do not want to accept that such things happened in Biblical times. But these problems stem from a weak view of God. The real problem then is not with miracles but with the whole concept of God. Once we are convinced about the existence of God then miracles are no problem. In fact it would be utterly astonishing if they did not exist. And the converse is also true... if we are convinced about miracles then, the existence of God is a natural conclusion!

Biblical miracles were never performed for personal prestige or to gain money or power. They are always performed for the benefit of others and for the highest of all motivations. Jesus Himself saw them as of paramount importance in declaring His deity to the world, as He told the Jewish leaders of His day:

> *I told you, and you do not believe. The works that I do in*
> *my Father's name, they bear witness to me.*
> *Jn 10:25*

> *Believe me that I am in the Father and the Father in me; or*
> *else believe me for the sake of the works themselves.*
> *Jn 14:11.*

The Nature of Christ's Miracles.

The miracles of Jesus were both frequent and varied. We mean by this that it was not the case that sometimes He could do miraculous things and sometimes not. There were never occasions when He set out to perform a miracle and had to give up because His magic wouldn't work.

Also it is notable that there was a tremendous variety to the miraculous things that Jesus could do. It was certainly not the case that the Lord had a few magic tricks up His sleeve and the five tricks were rotated as He performed them in different towns. There was a tremendous variety to the amazing signs which Jesus seemed able to perform at will.

Such miracles are usually classified into the following main groups:-

1. Power over nature.

On one occasion the disciples were crossing the Sea of Galilee in a boat when Jesus came to them walking upon the water. This displayed power over gravity, one of the most fundamental of all laws of Nature. Yet Jesus as Lord of this Creation displayed His mastery over it. He fed the 5000, turned the water into wine, stilled the storm and did all manner of things that displayed His mastery over His creation.

2. Power over disease.

One accusation which has been made by many concerning the healing miracles is that they must have been chiefly over psychosomatic illnesses. Indeed much of the modern "faith healings" would appear to fall into this category. And yet is that true of the healing miracles of Jesus? Lepers who had been diagnosed as suffering from the disease and banished to live outside society were cleansed at his command. They went away and were cleansed as they walked! Psychosomatic? Never. Then there were clear-cut cases of healing congenital disease, such as the man born blind (John 9). He had been blind from birth. His family knew it, his neighbors knew it, the whole town knew it. Indeed it is commented in the chapter itself:

> *Never since the world began has it been heard that any one opened the eyes of a man born blind. If this man were not from God, he could do nothing. Jn 9:32-33*

But he went to the pool and came back seeing at the simple word of Jesus. Another example of this most common type of miracle that Jesus performed is His healing of the servant of a centurion who lived in Capernaum.

> *⁵ As he entered Capernaum, a centurion came forward to him, beseeching him ⁶ and saying, "Lord, my servant is lying paralyzed at home, in terrible distress." ⁷ And he said to him, "I will come and heal him." ⁸ But the centurion answered*

*him, "Lord, I am not worthy to have you come under my
roof; but only say the word, and my servant will be healed.
⁹ For I am a man under authority, with soldiers under me;
and I say to one, 'Go,' and he goes, and to another, 'Come,'
and he comes, and to my slave, 'Do this,' and he does it." ¹⁰
When Jesus heard him, he marveled, and said to those who
followed him, "Truly, I say to you, not even in Israel have I
found such faith. ¹¹ I tell you, many will come from east and
west and sit at table with Abraham, Isaac, and Jacob in the
kingdom of heaven, ¹² while the sons of the kingdom will be
thrown into the outer darkness; there men will weep and
gnash their teeth." ¹³ And to the centurion Jesus said, "Go; be
it done for you as you have believed." And the servant was
healed at that very moment.
Matt 8:5-13.*

What was it that endeared Jesus to so many? What was it that
gathered such crowds wherever He went? It was that His ability to heal
diseases that no doctor could cure, and no medicine could help.

3.   Power over demons.

It is difficult for us to tune into this kind of miracle for we have
no personal experience of it. Most of us have encountered and even
experienced ill health before, but when the Bible talks about Jesus
casting out demons it is difficult for us to imagine this or picture it in
our minds.

*¹ They came to the other side of the sea, to the country of the
Gerasenes. ² And when he had come out of the boat, there
met him out of the tombs a man with an unclean spirit, ³
who lived among the tombs; and no one could bind him any
more, even with a chain; ⁴ for he had often been bound with
fetters and chains, but the chains he wrenched apart, and
the fetters he broke in pieces; and no one had the strength to
subdue him. ⁵ Night and day among the tombs and on the
mountains he was always crying out, and bruising himself
with stones. ⁶ And when he saw Jesus from afar, he ran and*

worshiped him; [7] and crying out with a loud voice, he said,
"What have you to do with me, Jesus, Son of the Most High
God? I adjure you by God, do not torment me." [8] For he had
said to him, "Come out of the man, you unclean spirit!" [9]
And Jesus asked him, "What is your name?" He replied,
"My name is Legion; for we are many." [10] And he begged
him eagerly not to send them out of the country. [11] Now a
great herd of swine was feeding there on the hillside; [12] and
they begged him, "Send us to the swine, let us enter them."
[13] So he gave them leave. And the unclean spirits came out,
and entered the swine; and the herd, numbering about two
thousand, rushed down the steep bank into the sea, and were
drowned in the sea. Mk 5:1-13

And yet in the ministry of Jesus it was commonplace... and in the ministry of the apostles following it was present if not as common... and we notice that in the writings of the epistles it seems to die out. Many scholars believe that the prevalence of demon possession at the time of the ministry of Jesus and the beginning of the church is just one symptom of the opposition of the devil to the setting up of God's kingdom. When in due season the kingdom was established, we see their interference diminish as Satan saw that the Spirit had been bestowed and his efforts were fruitless. Demons almost certainly do not act in the same way today, God would not permit anyone or anything to so take control of us that we were not responsible for our own actions any longer. But nevertheless such demons were very active in the time of Christ and He exhibited absolute authority over them.

4. Power over material things.

Jesus showed His power over the material universe in a number of ways. One example was when Jesus multiplied the five loaves and two fishes until there was enough food to feed five thousand men, besides women and children.

[13] Now when Jesus heard this, he withdrew from there in
a boat to a lonely place apart. But when the crowds heard
it, they followed him on foot from the towns. [14] As he went

ashore he saw a great throng; and he had compassion on them, and healed their sick. [15] When it was evening, the disciples came to him and said, "This is a lonely place, and the day is now over; send the crowds away to go into the villages and buy food for themselves." [16] Jesus said, "They need not go away; you give them something to eat." [17] They said to him, "We have only five loaves here and two fish." [18] And he said, "Bring them here to me." [19] Then he ordered the crowds to sit down on the grass; and taking the five loaves and the two fish he looked up to heaven, and blessed, and broke and gave the loaves to the disciples, and the disciples gave them to the crowds. [20] And they all ate and were satisfied. And they took up twelve baskets full of the broken pieces left over. [21] And those who ate were about five thousand men, besides women and children. Matt 14:13-21.

Another example would be turning water into wine at the wedding feast in Cana (in John ch 2).

5.   Power over death.

Perhaps the most startling sign of all was the power displayed by Jesus over death itself. We know that on hearing of the illness of Lazarus His friend, Jesus delayed His journey to Bethany till after Lazarus had died. And, even though Lazarus had been dead in the tomb four days, Jesus called him forth and he came walking from the tomb. See Jn 11:1-44.

The Importance of the Miracles.

These miraculous signs were regarded by Jesus to be important. They were the means by which the validity of His ministry was demonstrated to the people. They were the means by which people would know that he had come from God and was the representation of God to the nation. Believe me because of the works that I do, said Jesus.

We should recall the following points about these miracles.

1. Firstly the miracles were done in public. They were not performed in secret before only one or two people who announced them to the world. Suppose all the miracles performed by Jesus had only ever been seen by Peter and John and we relied wholly on their testimony. We would expect the skeptics to have a field day with that. But they are validated on the basis of eye-witness testimony of many people. These things were not done in a corner, but in full view of the multitudes. Men who had been lame beggars all their lives, stood and leapt and ran. There was no argument. The man blind from birth, saw and walked home seeing. None could deny it.

2. Secondly we note that when the opponents and enemies of Jesus wished to attack Him, they did not say that He never performed miracles. That was beyond question. What they said was that He must have done it by the power of the devil.

   Then a blind and dumb demoniac was brought to him, and he healed him, so that the dumb man spoke and saw. And all the people were amazed and said, Can this be the Son of David?" But when the Pharisees heard it they said, "It is only by Beelzebul, the prince of demons, that this man casts out demons." Matt 12:22-24.

   This showed that they could not attack the veracity of the signs themselves. You see it is one thing to ask people to believe in miracles because some people claim to have witnessed them. But it is quite another to have the concrete proof standing in front of you in the person of a blind man given sight, a leper cleansed, or a lame man who now leaps and runs.

3. Thirdly, we note that some miracles were performed in the presence of unbelievers. It is notable that in modern times, events which are claimed as miracles are not performed in the presence of the skeptic. But people were compelled to believe in Jesus against their will by the evidence of their own eyes and ears. It was not a requirement for Jesus that

to witness one of his miracles you had to first of all be a believer. It is commonplace in counterfeit miracles and miracle-workers of today that you have to be a believer before you can witness. And further, if you were to witness it and not be convinced that a miracle has taken place, then one is told that the problem is with oneself. The problem is that you do not have enough faith to perceive the miracle. There was none of that nonsense with Jesus. Skeptic and believer alike were convinced that a miracle had taken place. They may disagree about the source of the power for it, but the fact of the miracle was not in dispute.

4. Fourthly, we note that there was the unconquerable testimony of the cured. You may recall that the triumphal entry of Jesus into Jerusalem was that which triggered the final opposition of the Jewish leaders and resulted in His crucifixion. What was it that gathered such crowds to welcome Him and to acclaim Him as the promised Messiah? You will note that it followed a few days after the resurrection of Lazarus. To fulfill the prophecy concerning the triumphal entry was very simple... it only required to raise someone from the dead. His is the classic case of a healing which could never be explained away as being psychosomatic. In John ch 9 what could they do with the man born blind for his testimony was plain...

So for the second time they called the man who had been blind, and said to him, "Give God the praise; we know that this man is a sinner." He answered, "Whether he is a sinner, I do not know; one thing I know, that I was blind, now I see." Jn 9:24-25.

When the great crowd of the Jews learned that he was there, they came, not only on account of Jesus but also to see Lazarus, whom He had raised from the dead. So the chief priests planned to put Lazarus also to death, because on account of him many of the Jews were going away and believing in Jesus. Jn 12:9-11.

Conclusion:

So you see that the miracles of Jesus are integral to the story. You cannot go through the story of Jesus and seek to remove all that is miraculous from it... for you would have nothing left. The miracles were an integral part of the ministry of Jesus, and all accepted that He performed such signs, both friend and foe alike.

When Nicodemus, who since he was one of the leaders of the Jews must be regarded as part of the opposition, came to Jesus by night, his conclusion should be noted:

> *This man came to Jesus by night and said to him, "Rabbi, we know that you are a teacher come from God; for no one can do these signs that you do, unless God is with him." Jn 3:2.*

Nicodemus was right. He had come to faith because of the signs, because of the miracles which Jesus did.

In closing, consider the case of Judas Iscariot. He had made up his mind to betray Jesus. What could have been more damaging than to give the low down, give the first hand evidence of all the tricks that Jesus had been pulling to fool the people. On this score, the lips of Judas are sealed. He had nothing to say. All he can do is tell the Jews where Jesus prayed.

I believe, because of the miracles of Jesus.

Chapter Seventeen

I Believe Because... The Testimony of Changed Lives

Perhaps we might be tempted to look at this chapter and think that it is a wee bit more subjective, rather than an objective proof. Since my initial training was in the sciences, it is a proof that once I would never have included at all. However there is an old adage which says that the "proof of the pudding is in the eating". What is the effect of Christianity in the lives of men and women?

There can be little doubt that the world will judge Christianity by its effect. And every evangelist will have his own stories to tell, of people whose lives have been turned around by the power of the gospel.

Naturally if you devote your life to sharing the gospel there will be disappointments. There will be some who never make the decision to put on the Lord. And there will be some who do not stay the course. However we are sustained by the fellowship of all those who do remain faithful to Christ and whose lives are revolutionized by the power of God working within.

We were looking through some old photographs with our grandchildren the other day and we came across an old photograph of my performing the baptism of a young man. I confess I had forgotten that I was the one who baptized him. My four year old grandson then asked, "Papa, how many people have you baptized?" I must confess that I was stumped at that. I have always felt that it was somehow unseemly to take a count, lest there should ever be a time that in my arrogance I should for a moment think that I had saved anyone rather than the grace of God and the blood of Christ. And so these moments of great victory I have rejoiced at and immediately dismissed from my mind lest I should glory in them in a personal sense. However, in moments of discouragement, and times of struggle I have sometimes wondered if it might be good to reflect back on thirty plus years of preaching the gospel. Perhaps remembering each one individually might be good. Perhaps there would be no sin in glorying, perhaps not for myself, but giving thanks. I am thankful for the times when I think that God has been able to use me as an inadequate instrument of His grace, bringing men and women out of darkness and into light. I had a conversation recently with a sister in Christ and she reminded me that I had baptized her some years earlier. I think she was surprised and perhaps a little offended that I seemed to have forgotten that. However the reason was simple. I must never boast as if the saving were my doing, nor keep a count as if the credit were mine. For salvation is of God and through the sacrifice of the Perfect Lamb of God.

Lesslie Newbigin said that when people come to the gateway of the church they cannot help but look beyond the gateway to see what the product of the church may be. When people embrace the gospel, what does it do for them, to them and with them? What is the end product of the gospel? This seems like a reasonable question. Are people changed? Are people helped? Is there a measurable or distinguishable effect of putting on the Lord Jesus?

There are of course notable characters in history who on becoming acquainted with the grace of God in Christ have gone through complete transformations in their lives. But perhaps it is more appropriate for me to speak of just a few of people whose lives have been changed before my eyes. Because this is not their own given personal testimony but my observations, I have changed the names of each, but the stories are real nonetheless.

I first met Grant at a psychiatric outpatient clinic in Glasgow. He was a young man experiencing terrible and life-limiting phobias. He used to walk for over an hour to get to the clinic because he could not bear to be on a bus with other passengers. His psychiatrist described him as socially phobic. Grant had started reading the Bible himself and was not understanding very much, just enough to add to his phobias. He was looking over his body to see if he had the mark of the beast anywhere on his body. His psychiatrist was an atheist but after some enquiry had called me in and asked if I was prepared to have a go at getting somewhere with Grant because nothing they were doing was getting anywhere fast. We met and read the Bible together and Grant came to know something of how much he was loved. At what cost the Father had reached out a loving hand to him. And after a struggle which lasted a few months, he was able to start attending church, sitting on a chair placed specially at the door and the door had to be left open for quick escape if the panic overcame him. But with patience and love, Grant one day made the great decision to become a Christian, to put on the Lord in baptism and to attend the Lord's Table. That was some 25 years ago or more and he is still being faithful to the Lord and to the Table. He still has struggles but he is deeply conscious of how much he has been helped in his life by the Lord. It was my privilege to introduce Grant to the Savior through the precious Word of the gospel, and knowing Jesus is that which makes the difference.

Dave was a young musician. His ambition in life was to be a successful singer-song-writer like Elton John. And though he did have great talent, it seemed that this ambition was unlikely to come to fruition. He wrote the songs, he performed well, but fame did not come knocking at the door no matter what he did. Being in that realm, there were always opportunities to become engaged in activity that the Christian should avoid, and the temptation was great. I had known Dave's family when he was a young boy and met him again as a young adult with no particular faith and spasmodic spiritual aspirations. I would go to his house every week to study the Bible with him with the hope of winning him over for Christ. There were times I went to his door and there was no answer. There were times when this happened that I formed the opinion that though the door was not opened, there was someone home. However with patience and steadfastness the home study continued for many months and in due course, something of the loveliness of Jesus penetrated into Dave's heart and he did indeed become a Christian. I had the privilege of baptizing him into Christ Jesus. Years later, Dave took me aside one day with a rather grave look on his face. "There is something I need to tell you Alastair," he said. He then proceeded to tell me that there were days when I came for the Bible study, that he was home and did not answer the door because the contrast was too great with the life he was living. There were tears in his eyes as he confessed this to me. I was then able to say to him, "I knew." This is the wonder of the grace of God, that while we were yet sinners, Christ died for us. His love and grace reaches out to us… and He is willing to grasp us to Himself, even before we are willing to give ourselves to Him. More than twenty years have passed and Dave is married to a fine Christian woman, has a son, and all three are faithful to Christ and faithful in worship. And who would have thought this of the aspiring pop star, and his unholy lifestyle. But the gospel changes things, and changes people. And changes them for the better.

Eric was a prisoner when I met him. He was incarcerated in Saughton Prison in Edinburgh, serving a life sentence for murder. Our first association was by means of correspondence as he studied a Bible correspondence course I offered at the time. There were a number of prisoners who were studying the course with varying degrees of interest. As I came to know Eric I discovered that he was convicted of murdering his wife on their honeymoon in Edinburgh in rather a notorious case, the wife having fallen to her death from Salisbury Crags, a well known feature of what is known locally as Arthur's Seat, a high hill, a volcanic plug in Holyrood Park in the city. The spot was a popular beauty spot in the middle of Scotland's capital city. Later we were to have Eric visit in our home and eat at our table. We had the privilege of having his mother come and stay with us as she came over to visit from her homeland, and though we spoke none of her language and she spoke none of ours, we did learn to communicate after a fashion. Eric was to spend 15 years in prison. The last I heard of him he was serving as a church minister in his homeland in Europe. Did the Word of God have any effect on his life? I think that is certain and demonstrable.

Time and space do not permit me to mention many others I have known whose lives have been touched and changed by the gospel. The woman who had been a hopeless alcoholic— changed by the gospel so that her home became a Christian home and I had the privilege of baptizing her husband into Christ. The woman who suffered mental illness and who had at best a fractured life, damaged by illness and broken and dysfunctional relationships. How wonderful to see her, like that man who met Jesus in the gospel records— sitting in her right mind, coherent and making sense out of her life and relationships. I had the privilege of seeing her reconciled with her children, performed her wedding, and was a welcome weekly guest in their home as we studied the Bible together. There are many other stories, some dramatic and some less so. There is one fact that seems to be undeniable. People are changed by the gospel. People are helped. There is a power at work which amounts to more than group dynamics in the local assembly. And perhaps the crowning of this argument is that I can see in my own life the unmistakable fingerprints of God in changing and molding me into a likeness, even an imperfect likeness due to the stubbornness of the clay at times, but a likeness nonetheless of His perfect character and holiness.

Essentially we shall reach a point when we have to say to people come and see for yourselves. There is an old Scottish saying that Christianity is better "felt than telt"! I am not sure I subscribe wholly to that philosophy but there must be an element of truth in there. People have to be encouraged to come and experience some of the majesty of drawing close to Jesus. There is an incident in the gospel records which suggests this.

> [35] *The next day again John was standing with two of his disciples;* [36] *and he looked at Jesus as he walked, and said, "Behold, the Lamb of God!"* [37] *The two disciples heard him say this, and they followed Jesus.* [38] *Jesus turned, and saw them following, and said to them, "What do you seek?" And they said to him, "Rabbi" (which means Teacher), "where are you staying?"* [39] *He said to them, "Come and see." They came and saw where he was staying; and they stayed with him that day, for it was about the tenth hour. John 1:35-39.*

These disciples of John the Baptist had to come and see for themselves the magnetism of the Master.

Perhaps the psalmist stated it most succinctly.

⁸ O taste and see that the LORD is good!
Happy is the man who takes refuge in him! Psalm 34:8.

One preacher of a previous generation was preaching one day when interrupted by a heckler. The man shouted out that atheism has done more good for the world than Christianity. The preacher replied with a challenge. You bring a hundred people here tomorrow night whose lives have been changed for the better by atheism and I will bring a hundred whose lives have been transformed by Christ. Needless to say, the heckler did not return the following night. It would be an easy matter to find a hundred Christians who would testify that their lives have been transformed by the Christ, and made more meaningful, given direction and purpose, impregnated with an inner peace and suffused with a matchless love. And surely this must count as some kind of proof.

I believe because of transformed lives.

Chapter Eighteen

Blessed are those who have not seen, and yet believe

IN THE WRITINGS OF PAUL the concept of preaching the gospel is seen as central to Paul's ministry, Paul's apostleship. And Paul's life is the preaching of the gospel. In Romans chapter 1, it is clearly stated in a great theme statement for the whole epistle that the gospel is the power of God to save... Paul devoted his life to the gospel and the preaching of the Word that brings life. The whole purpose of his life is to bring about the obedience of faith by the preaching of the gospel.

> *[16] For I am not ashamed of the gospel: it is the power of God for salvation to every one who has faith, to the Jew first and also to the Greek. Rom 1:16-17.*

> *[1] Paul, a servant of Jesus Christ, called to be an apostle, set apart for the gospel of God [2] which he promised beforehand through his prophets in the holy scriptures, [3] the gospel concerning his Son, who was descended from David according to the flesh [4] and designated Son of God in power according to the Spirit of holiness by his resurrection from the dead, Jesus Christ our Lord, [5] through whom we have received grace and apostleship to bring about the obedience of faith for the sake of his name among all the nations, [6]*

211

including yourselves who are called to belong to Jesus Christ;
Rom 1:1-6

Why is gospel sharing given such a prominent place in the life of the new church? Paul is appointed as apostle to the Gentiles, and Paul sees it as absolutely central to his life and to the life of the church. Planting the seed of the Word of God brings us from death to life... we are born anew by the implanted Word of God . As Peterson puts in the Message version:

> *Your new life is not like your old life. Your old birth came*
> *from mortal sperm; your new birth comes from God's living*
> *Word. Just think: a life conceived by God himself! That's why*
> *the prophet said,*
> *The old life is a grass life,*
> *its beauty as short-lived as wildflowers;*
> *Grass dries up, flowers droop,*
> *God's Word goes on and on forever.*
> *This is the Word that conceived the new life in you.*
> *1 Peter 1:23-25*

When the Word of Christ is planted in our hearts, it is a seed that bursts forth into life. The Word is the sword of the Spirit and the Spirit brings life and hence the new birth occurs. The key to everything is listening to the story of Jesus.

The Word of the gospel is the Word about the Word who was in the beginning with God and who was God, the Word who became flesh and dwelt among us and we beheld His glory, glory as of the only Son of the Heavenly Father.

And everything depends upon faith. And how is this faith to be established? In John chapter 20, Thomas is confronted with the eyewitness testimony of his fellow disciples. We have seen the Lord. He was here! But Thomas struggled with this message which challenged his faith and demanded that he should believe a truth which seemed too wonderful to be true. Thomas doubted. Thomas would not believe unless he saw the nail prints in His hands, unless he saw the wound in His side. Then Jesus appeared before Thomas so that he could see and believe.

Thomas was called upon to believe because of the evidence of his own eyes. He saw Jesus and he believed. And this after all was what happened with the other apostles. They became eyewitnesses of His resurrection and believed.

But Thomas could not believe because of testimony and needed the eyewitness experience before he would believe. But we are not in this situation. It would seem most unlikely that the Lord Himself will appear before us in order that we might see. Indeed Jesus addressed this very issue when speaking to Thomas. *Blessed are those who have not seen and yet believe.* And on this basis every person who ever became a Christian after this time has become a Christian because of a narrative about the Christ. They responded to a remarkable story. It is an historical story, a true story. It is powerful story, a gospel story. It is gospel truth. They have heard the story and come to faith.

And how is it that they are to believe? It is to do with the story that has been written down. John said that these things concerning the signs in the gospel of John were written in order that we might believe that Jesus is the Christ and that in believing we would have life in His name (Jn 20:30-31).

Studying the signs and really interacting with the text is a faith building experience and men and women are brought to faith by it. Why should this surprise us? It is what the text claims for itself. Paul says in another text that faith comes by hearing and hearing the preaching of Christ

> *[14] But how are men to call upon him in whom they have not believed? And how are they to believe in him of whom they have never heard? And how are they to hear without a preacher? [15] And how can men preach unless they are sent? As it is written, "How beautiful are the feet of those who preach good news!" [16] But they have not all obeyed the gospel; for Isaiah says, "Lord, who has believed what he has heard from us?" [17] So faith comes from what is heard, and what is heard comes by the preaching of Christ. Rom 10:14-17*

And hence the work of evangelism does not depend on clever gimmicks, or electronic wizardry of some kind but it depends on the Word of God like it always has. It does not even depend upon the consummate skill of the evangelist (story teller). It depends upon getting people to engage with the text of the gospel. It depends upon drinking in the gospel message and faith comes like it always has. It depends upon the story and not the storyteller.

Jesus promised that when the Son of Man is lifted up, He would draw all men to Himself (Jn 12:31). He still does. How many Christians today are scared stiff of becoming involved in the process of evangelism and spend a great deal of effort finding excuses as to why they could not possibly do so. It is the work of the evangelist, the preacher, the elder, the gifted, the learned— indeed just about anyone except me. Why is this the case? It is a truth that the church today is not growing as it did in the first few chapters of Acts. And it is noticeable that the church today is not as engaged in the process of telling the story of Jesus as the church in the New Testament. Why is that?

Is it because we are afraid of making mistakes? Possibly. But who is there alive who does not make mistakes? Is it because we feel that we are too unholy to be engaged in such a holy process? Perhaps this is a much more brutally honest answer. If we put ourselves in the front line, is it possible that our spiritual inadequacies will come under the spot light and we may embarrass ourselves, and the church. I think if that is the case then there are more spiritual problems evident than the lack of evangelistic enthusiasm and we need to really engage in some serious self-examination. We may need to resolve issues to get our spiritual lives on track, not just for the sake of congregational evangelism but also for the sake of our own spiritual development as Christians.

There can be little doubt that in the early church the whole church was involved in the evangelism process. Every member became an ambassador. Look at the events of the end of Acts chapter seven and beginning of Acts chapter eight. Who were scattered by this persecution? Everyone except the apostles. Who were engaged in the telling of the story? Those who were scattered. It was not a matter of specialism, that some might be engaged in building care maintenance, some in Bible class teaching and there might be some in the congregation that would inevitably end up in the evangelism specialty.

When the church was most successfully growing, and the church was under the administration of inspired apostles, every Christian was engaged in the telling business. Not all need to be engaged in the role of public preaching and teaching. Not every Christian is suitably blessed with that kind of talent or gift. The idea of specialisms and using each man's talent where appropriate in the kingdom is a good one. But I think it becomes clear that the telling of the good news is exempt from the specialisms approach. We have all been blessed and saved by the blood of the Word who became flesh, and all need to be capable of telling good news. No special training is really necessary, no certification in the specialist course in telling the story is required, what is needed is excitement about the story we have learned. The story has changed my life. Can I tell you about it? Can I point you to the story so you can learn it too? There are those who would point to the approach of every Christian identifying a ministry they can become engaged in. And I am one of those preachers who has preached this. But telling the story is something for every Christian too. Do you see a ministry you can perform? Great! Do it with all your might but telling the story of the gospel is inherent in becoming a Christian. Note what Paul had to say in Rom 10:8-10.

> *8 But what does it say? The word is near you, on your lips and in your heart (that is, the word of faith which we preach); 9 because, if you confess with your lips that Jesus is Lord and believe in your heart that God raised him from the dead, you will be saved. 10 For man believes with his heart and so is justified, and he confesses with his lips and so is saved.*

Confessing Christ is all bound up in the story of my redemption… I am saved to tell.

Maybe there are specialisms in the telling process. Inviting people to come to church and participate in the worship experience, maybe that is a specialism. Talking to neighbors and friends and inviting them to join in a home Bible study, maybe that is a specialism.

Churches that are growing are churches where the majority of the membership are engaged in some way in the business of telling the story of Jesus.

Churches that are not growing are churches were the majority think that a small dedicated group of people, or worse, one man only, should be involved in the telling process because that is their specialism, or his specialism not mine.

Peter tells us that we have been bought by the blood of Christ *that* we might tell the goodness of God. Look at how Peterson in The Message renders this passage:

> *But you are the ones chosen by God, chosen for the high calling of priestly work, chosen to be a holy people, God's instruments to do his work and speak out for him, to tell others of the night-and-day difference he made for you— from nothing to something, from rejected to accepted. 1 Peter 2:9-10*

One way of expressing this passage would be to say that we are saved to tell. But note please that this is within the scope of most Christians. Could you tell someone with some excitement how things unfolded in the most popular soap opera last night? Could you tell someone with some excitement what happened in last night's big game? Could you tell someone of the wonderful family wedding you attended last weekend? If you could tell these exciting stories, then you can tell the most exciting story of all.

As we consider what had been said in this volume, it is good to reflect on the central issues. We began by examining the world-view perspective of the Christian and contrasting this with the worldview of the rest of society. The following observations may be made:

1. That the Christian worldview informs our sense of identity. That we view ourselves in light of the faith narrative that Scripture presents. We are defined by the faith narrative of Creation, Fall, Redemption, Sanctification and Glorification.

2. This is in sharp contrast with the nihilistic picture presented by a Darwinian approach, which colors much of the world of education and modern society as a whole. This views our existence as a cosmic accident having no purpose, no direction and no destiny. We are doomed to go out of existence and there is no hope. Of necessity, this will radically affect the worldview. It will also affect how the gospel is viewed.

3. This leaves us with a puzzle as to how best communicate the gospel to a world that views everything radically differently from the Christian perspective. How can we communicate the gospel to a lost world with a Darwinian worldview?

4. It may seem logical to go onto the offensive with a radical program of Christian evidences, fulfilled prophecies, scientific foreknowledge and other "proofs" of the faith position. And yet this program of radical education is in itself not any guarantee of effective communication of the hope of the gospel.

5. We saw that the solution suggested in Scripture is that we must present not a system of education or philosophy but a Person. It is in getting to know Jesus that our way of thinking is changed and we receive what Paul in the epistle to the Romans called a "new mind" (Rom 12:1-2). It is in getting to know Jesus that our perspective is changed. We may still have to address some issues. But the major point is that knowing Jesus changes our worldview, and makes faith possible. Faith comes by hearing and hearing the good news of Christ. It is the gospel which is the power of God unto salvation!

6. We come to know Jesus from our introduction to Him in the gospel records. These things are written that we might believe. And hence it is by becoming immersed in the Word that we come to see Him and to know Him. But is it a case of just reading the Bible? We suggested that it is reading the Bible but it is reading it in a deeper

way. It will be in truly engaging with the text that we find ourselves immersed in the story of Jesus and coming to know Him personally. Engaging with the text means seeing ourselves in the story and the story of Jesus becoming our story.

7. It was suggested in this volume that we can be introduced to Jesus through the message of the fourth gospel.

8. We see that the fourth gospel is based on an examination of seven signs through which Jesus demonstrated that He truly is the Word who was in the beginning with God and who was God, who became flesh and dwelt among us and we beheld His glory, glory as of the only Son from the Father. And through this Word, we are born again of that imperishable seed which is the Word of God and find our new identity in Christ. And the pointless non-existence of the man of the flesh is lost in the new identity of the man of the Spirit, and we find our hope, our destiny in Him.

We reach out to the world with a great message and a great challenge. If worldly man would come and meet Jesus then everything will be changed. He will not view the world in the same way (his worldview will be radically altered). He will not view God in the same way (he will see with crystal clarity the fulness of deity for the fulness of deity dwelt in Him). He will not view himself or life in the same way, for he will come to fulness of life in Him.

We come to ask the question that Jesus asked the Pharisees.

> *⁴¹ Now while the Pharisees were gathered together, Jesus asked them a question, ⁴² saying, "What do you think of the Christ? Whose son is he?" Matt 22:41-42.*

And perhaps this is the only really important question in the world. With reference to the Christ, whose Son is He?

The whole of the New Testament is written that we might reach definite conclusions. The gospel records are written that we might see a great eternal truth concerning this Jesus. He is Son of David. He is the promised King. He whom the world has awaited has come. He reigns, as Messiah King was meant to do. And the only questionable thing is whether you shall be part of His great Messianic kingdom. Shall we each enthrone Him? Shall we make Him King of our hearts and our lives? And if that marvelous transaction is made, then we will not walk in darkness but have the light of life.

He is Son of God. He is the Word who was in the beginning with God and who was God. He became flesh as the greatest expression of the grace of God and love of Christ, and dwelt among us and we beheld His glory. Since He is the Son of God, then let us worship and adore Him as the Savior of our souls.

Printed in the United Kingdom by
Lightning Source UK Ltd., Milton Keynes
136623UK00002B/52/P